PERGAMON RUSSIAN CHESS SERIES

Chess in the Eighties

PERGAMON RUSSIAN CHESS SERIES

General Editor: KENNETH P. NEAT
Executive Editor: MARTIN J. RICHARDSON

AVERBAKH, Y.
Chess Endings: Essential Knowledge

BOTVINNIK, M. M.
Achieving the Aim
Anatoly Karpov: His Road to the World Championship
Selected Games 1967–70

ESTRIN, Y. and PANOV, V. N.
Comprehensive Chess Openings

KARPOV, A. and GIK, Y.
Chess Kaleidoscope

KARPOV, A. and ROSHAL, A.
Anatoly Karpov: Chess is My Life

LIVSHITZ, A.
Test Your Chess IQ, Books 1 & 2

NEISHTADT, Y.
Catastrophe in the Opening

POLUGAYEVSKY, L.
Grandmaster Preparation

SUETIN, A. S.
Modern Chess Opening Theory

SUETIN, A. S.
Three Steps to Chess Mastery

TAL, M., CHEPIZHNY, V. and ROSHAL, A.
Montreal 1979: Tournament of Stars

Chess in the Eighties

by

D. BRONSTEIN and G. SMOLYAN

Translated by

KENNETH P. NEAT

PERGAMON PRESS

OXFORD · NEW YORK · TORONTO · SYDNEY · PARIS · FRANKFURT

U.K.	Pergamon Press Ltd., Headington Hill Hall, Oxford OX3 0BW, England
U.S.A.	Pergamon Press Inc., Maxwell House, Fairview Park, Elmsford, New York 10523, U.S.A.
CANADA	Pergamon Press Canada Ltd., Suite 104, 150 Consumers Road, Willowdale, Ontario M2J 189, Canada
AUSTRALIA	Pergamon Press (Aust.) Pty. Ltd., P. O. Box 544, Potts Point, N.S.W. 2011, Australia
FRANCE	Pergamon Press SARL, 24 rue des Ecoles, 75240 Paris, Cedex 05, France
FEDERAL REPUBLIC OF GERMANY	Pergamon Press GmbH, 6242 Kronberg-Taunus, Hammerweg 6, Federal Republic of Germany

English translation copyright © 1982 K. P. Neat

First English edition 1982

British Library Cataloguing in Publication Data

Bronstein, D
   Chess in the Eighties. — (Pergamon Russian chess series)
   1. Chess — Addresses, essays, lectures
   I. Title   II. Smolyan, G
   794.1   G1451
   ISBN 0-08-024126-3 Hard Cover
   LC 81—82526

This edition is a translation of *Prekrasnyi i yarostnyi mir* published by Znanie, 1978

Printed in Hungary by Franklin Printing House

To the memory of Paul Petrovich Keres,
sportsman, artist and citizen

Contents

To Our Reader

IT IS not possible to accommodate the content of this book in a short title, but a few words will be sufficient to convey the position of the authors, or at least their basic idea. We will be talking here about a unique phenomenon in our spiritual life—modern-day chess, and will resort to a variety of means to reveal the different aspects of this beautiful and frenzied world. And no matter what we have used—be it accounts of events from the history of chess or sociological studies, the results of psychology research or of mathematical modelling, the reflections of a journalist or the fantasy of a literary man—we have attempted to demonstrate the great social, moral and aesthetic importance of chess. Like millions of other people, we love chess for its happy ability to bestow the joy of intellectual intercourse and of vivid creative experience. It is from this stand-point that we discuss the various aspects of chess life, and we attempt to do this frankly, without avoiding any complex or thorny questions.

What is chess? A world of artefacts, a world of contrived complexity, but crammed with very real feelings, and full of alarms and hopes? A miraculous combination of sport and art, of competition and creativity, of will-power and thought, a combination in which victory is valued highly, and in which unfading art rises above the reality of competitive life? A pastime for old-age pensioners, comfortably ensconced on a park bench, and a lesson in self-knowledge for young pioneers? A game of millions, a mass use of spare time, an amusement, a part-time education, and a profession in big-time sport, with its organizations, press, science, customs and enthusiasts?

Chess is all of these.

Films, plays and ballets about chess, dissertations and university degrees, honorary titles, individual ratings, decorations and diplomas of all denominations, awards, cups, medals, badges and stamps. Champions of the world and of continents, individual, team, correspondence, men's, ladies', student, youth and children's events, championships of countries, towns, districts, ministries, institutes, factories, schools, ships, and polar expeditions on ice-floes. Family evenings at the chess board. Chess schools, courses on television, tours by popular champions, simultaneous displays, demonstrations, living chess, and the endless merry-go-round of elimination events at all levels of mastery. Chess columns in newspapers and magazines, problem and study-solving competitions. And books, books, books about chess, about chess players, about tournaments and matches. . . .

Yes, this is all chess. A game of people, about which it seems that everyone knows everything, and. . . no one knows anything.

The authors see the constantly and rapidly growing interest of the public in chess, and also know that literature on chess is growing rapidly.

This is extremely pleasing—for many reasons, and if only for the fact that one of the authors has devoted the whole of his life to chess. But it is also worrying—this stream of books and articles is dominated by special chess publications, which maintain the traditional genre of sports journalism. On the other hand, there are scant few works devoted to research into chess as an element of culture, and this is one of the motives which has persuaded us to take up the pen. The other, perhaps more important one, is that we wish to convey to our reader the feeling of disquiet with which we are possessed, at the infiltration into chess of the spirit of pragmatism, rationalism, and banal drudgery, generated by the atmosphere of fierce competition in big-time chess, which is perhaps a reflection of other, deeper mechanisms of modern cultural life. We think that this tendency threatens serious dangers for chess art, and for the high moral and cultural content of our favourite game.

Of course, the struggle between the rationalistic tendency, and the creative and artistic one, has not just recently begun, as many pages of chess history will testify. It is not denied that chess art develops from mass practice, and that without rational, dull, ordinary and banal games we would not be able to distinguish outstanding creative achievements.

But it appears to us that in recent years the view of chess as a high form of art has begun to make way for something else. Nowadays we are more proud of competitive achievements, and are barely concerned with the creative content of these achievements. We have begun talking about chess as of a branch of big-time sport, which exerts a deep and pervasive influence on the cultural leisure of millions of people. And this raises numerous questions, connected in particular with the interpretation of the spiritual values of our life, and with the moral upbringing of the young.

The authors also wish to raise a little above the ordinary the difficult profession of the chess player, of victorious and defeated champions, heroes of the sporting press, grandmasters and masters, who have chosen the 64-square board for the testing of their talent, people who live in big-time sport, in a world of tremendous effort and of great exertion of man's spiritual and physical potential. And if from our modest jottings the reader can sense how in the lives of these people, as if in the fragments of a gigantic mirror, the beautiful and frenzied world of big-time chess is reflected, we will be happy.

Chess is a unique and many-sided phenomenon. This special world of human activity arises from a thousand truths and a thousand caprices. To analyse this world is extremely difficult, but also highly tempting. Here it is easy to depart from the solid foundation of facts, and to head for the fantasy of supposition. It is for this reason that there is so much in our remarks which is subjective and debatable. For, as Ambrose Bierce said, discussion is merely a means of convincing your opponent of the error of his ways.

CHAPTER 1.

The World of Big-Time Sport

THE ISSUE of whether or not chess belongs to sport is one which has long been debated. Questions of this type are asked by journalists, and probably not one of the top chess players, especially the World Champions, would be able to avoid difficulties in seeking a compromise reply. In prefaces to games collections and other books, and in newspaper interviews, people who in the eyes of the rest have come to understand chess to its last depths, have weighed up more or less painstakingly the portions falling to the lot of game, sport, art, science and creativity. Much has depended on the mood, the problem and... the era.

In the preface to his *Chess Manual*, in 1926 Emanuel Lasker openly stated: "Here is presented the idea of the old game of chess, an idea which has given it the strength to exist through several centuries.... This is the idea of the struggle...." And in his splendid (although naive in its sociological aspects by present-day standards) booklet, *Steinitz i Lasker*, Mikhail Levidov carried on this idea through the lives and games of the first two World Champions. But in the same nineteen thirties A. F. Ilyin-Zhenevsky wrote that "the international workers' chess movement is acquiring an unprecedented scale and strength, and will produce examples of artistic play such as have never been seen by the world since the appearance of chess on this earth." Under the slogan "make room for chess and draughts in the working environment", the competitive factor was, naturally, of secondary importance. Chess is a cultural and socially beneficial game, wrote Professor of Psychology

A. P. Nechayev, but he promptly added that it is "an example of a struggle, in which the element of enmity is reduced to the minimum."

Let us be tolerant towards the authors of that time, although the
"hotch-potch of definitions", as Mikhail Botvinnik expressed it, is retained even today. In our time this author has reduced the components
of the hotch-potch, and has given the following formulation: "Chess
is always a game, which sometimes becomes an art". Time passes, and
the emphasis shifts unconditionally. "This argument is endless: what
is chess—sport, art or science? For me it is both the one, and the other,
and the third. But today chess is of course first and foremost a sport",
writes Anatoly Karpov. But after the exhausting Final Candidates'
Match in 1974, Karpov added in a television interview: "Chess is a cruel
type of sport. In it the weight of victory and defeat lies on the shoulders of
one man. . . . When you play well and lose, it's terrible." The American
grandmaster Reuben Fine remarked in plain terms: "Chess is a sport,
just like basketball or tennis. You propel the ball about until you win
a point. You move the pieces until you find a weak square."

It is not a matter of definitions, of course, but of those tendencies
which are developing in the existence of chess organizations, in chess on
a mass scale, and in chess at a high professional level.

Here are some characteristic traits. In all the material devoted to the
50th Anniversary of the International Chess Federation in 1974, it is
stated that its authority and influence are associated with the fact that,
under its patronage, during the post-war years the strongest chess player
in the world has been determined, and that this always "draws particular
attention and provokes the interest of millions of people." In an interview, the FIDE President Max Euwe emphasized this, in speaking
about the tasks of the Jubilee Congress: "The main attention of the
International Federation Congress must be concentrated on the system of
conducting the World Championship." This is no accident. The organization of events, the perfecting of their rules and regulations, and the
introduction of the system of individual coefficients worked out by Árpád
Éló—these are the three main directions of activity of FIDE. At the
same time FIDE has never called anything in the nature of an international symposium on questions of chess creativity, nor has it attempted

to stimulate creative achievement by the establishment of international prizes or by any other means....

Let us see how the chess year is summed up. Look up any editorial in the New Year issue of *64* for the past 4–5 years. A list is given of victories in events, a few isolated failures, and complaints about the increasing average age of the USSR team—this is the past year. For the coming year—a programme of events and hopes for competitive success.

Sports organizations and chess federations are worried in particular about the slow rate at which our leading players are being replaced. This provokes respect, and we can only welcome the opening in Moscow, on Izmailovsky Boulevard, in boarding school No.9, of chess as a specialized subject. It is possible that, out of these first eleven lads, who gain top marks for chess along with geography and physics, young grandmasters will develop. But it has to be frankly admitted that the popularity of chess is closely linked to the question of whether or not a match for the World Championship has taken place, and this gives rise to a certain concern.

We will not develop these theses any further. Much will already be understandable. After all, we are not "selecting" our material impartially, although to show the activity of chess organizations, directed towards the development of chess as an art, is much more complicated.

Chess tournaments and matches, especially those concerned with the battle for the World Championship, are events of great public importance. It is doubtful whether anyone would dispute this. In recent years, public interest in chess as a sport has particularly increased. Wide coverage in the press and on television, participation in events with prizes and the opportunity to travel and see the world, have aroused a keen interest in chess, and, unfortunately, one that is not always impartial.

How times change! In the nineteenth century the spectator was impressed by the "amateur", and not the professional. Chess, remarks Levidov, is an "amusement", unworthy of being the profession of a "serious" person. Today the public is impressed by a high level of mastery, by a high degree of professionalism.

This is understandable, because today the standard of achievement in sport is so high, and demands such colossal expenditure of time and energy, that it is not easy for a great sportsman to have any other occupation.

It should be emphasized that professionalism in big-time sport, as an essential condition for a high degree of mastery and for the achievement of the highest successes, including in chess, is characteristic both of our amateur sport, as well as of Western professionally commercial sport. And today chess has entered firmly into our spiritual life, namely as a form of sport, carrying out fully its cultural and educational functions.

The dilettante differs from the specialist, Helmholtz once said, only in that he lacks a reliable working method, and that, therefore, for the most part he is unable to test the importance of a suddenly occurring idea, evaluate it, and put it into effect. This was said about the scientist, but is also characteristic of any other activity. The "reliable working method" of a grandmaster or master must be constantly at a high level, and this can be attained only by the special organization of his life and work. For this reason, perhaps, the requirements today for a high level of mastery are seen most distinctly in the scale and organization of a grandmaster's or master's preparation for events. There are chances of success only for him who is able to shut himself off from everything extraneous to chess, who has grasped the scientific principles of training, who has tempered his health and will-power, and who is well versed in the modern team method of preparation. It is teams of specialists—trainers, seconds and helpers—who have replaced the intellectual recluses of earlier decades. And these teams work for several hours every day. "Everything depends on each individual in isolation," Ostap Bender[1] once proclaimed. Even that well-known fair-haired young man in the third row would play much worse today, if he didn't have a dark-haired trainer. It cannot be otherwise. How can you seek a continuation in a variation well known to everyone, which will promise at least some chances? How do you yourself avoid being caught in a prepared variation? How and when are you to play through those thousands of games played during the past year in dozens of tournaments and matches? How do you

---

[1] The main character in Ilf and Petrov's *Twelve Chairs;* a scene from the novel is also reflected in the next sentence (K. P. N.).

safeguard yourself against a possibly chance incorrect evaluation? The intensive and strenuous work of several persons is some guarantee of a reply to all these questions. Some guarantee, because it may still suddenly happen that you are caught in a prepared variation, and the game is won by the opponent in advance.

The new style of "ensuring victory by home team preparation" was perhaps first seen at Göteborg in 1955, when three Argentinians—Najdorf, Panno and Pilnik—lost their games in one round, against Keres, Geller and Spassky respectively, using one and the same prepared variation of the Sicilian Defence. At that time, joint analysis in preparing for a tournament or an individual game was not an especially common phenomenon. But today it is the norm. It is professional preparation, and its features can be seen in events at much lower level.

With the advent of "mass" home preparation, chess at master level has been transformed into a competition, not so much of talent, intuition and fantasy, so much as knowledge, memory and factors of preparation. The modern master possesses such experience, that he hardly requires to make considerable efforts to play from the first move for a draw. Of course, no one is insured against the fact that, in the event of a loss, all the enormous amount of preparatory work can come to nothing. Moreover, if it should find its way into print (and in practice nowadays the games from all events of any sort of importance are published), this once-lost game is lost repeatedly against all probable future opponents. The situation is aggravated by the fact that, through the mechanism of competitive elimination, this one single lost game can play a serious role in the fate of a master. "A chance draw with an outsider can prove very costly, and for three whole years can displace a grandmaster, who most of all deserves the right to meet the World Champion in a deciding match," was the statement made after his victory in the 1973 Interzonal Tournament in Brazil by Henrique Mecking. There are no doubt many masters who think likewise.

Competitive elimination, which should embody the principles of the highest levels of justice, is in modern chess cruel, and therefore... unjust. Isn't it cruel that you should lose a game because of a single mistake after $4\frac{1}{2}$ hours of intensive effort? Perhaps it was for this reason that the great humanist Einstein did not like chess. With the present-day elimination system in chess, as, however, in other forms of sports competitions, the element of chance, the caprice of the draw and of luck are frequently of no less importance than the level of mastery. This is one of the aspects of modern big-time sport. In it the one clearly defined criterion of effectiveness, of selection, of success, is victory. We cannot help but recall the apt remark made by Norman Weiner:

"In draughts and in chess this criterion [the criterion of effectiveness—*the authors*] reduces to winning, achieved according to the prescribed rules in force. These rules, which differ radically *from norms of benevolence* [Weiner's italics—*the authors*], are simple and merciless. This does not provoke doubts even among those gifted children who are capable of grasping the spirit of these rules, by fleetingly following the events developing on the chess board. The player may sometimes experience serious doubts regarding the choice of the best way to win, but he has not the slightest doubt as to whether he has to win or to lose."

This is why it is to be regretted that the first Champion of the World, Wilhelm Steinitz, called himself Champion, and did not have the sense to call himself Laureat. Then perhaps beauty of solution, risk, fantasy and daring would have been valued more highly in chess, there would not have been those prolonged matches, tiring for everyone, where it is important to conserve one's strength and wait for mistakes by the opponent, and where he who first takes a risk loses, and there would not have been those unattractive, simply tedious games. Of course, this is a complex question, touching on the global organization of events, the lives of chess players, and, probably, the fate of chess as a sport. That about which we are writing is an extreme point of view. We do this openly and deliberately, and will return again to a discussion of these ideas. It is not possible, surely, to give up the aesthetics of chess to composition, and for the practical game to retain only the competitive result! After all, the cultural-historical value of chess lies in its deep aesthetic effect, which is different, in our opinion, from the experience and rivalry of victory or defeat.

Whether one regrets it or not, it has to be admitted that the competitive element in modern chess "forgets" about everything else. Even the brilliancy prize is received by the winner alone, and no one ponders over the fact that a game is the product of the creativity of both players. Today it is impossible to imagine a tournament in which all the participants would play just one sharp opening, say, the Evans Gambit, with alternate colours. And yet 100 years ago such a tournament was staged. We will not, however, grumble and pine for the old days, and will regard with understanding the fact that chess organizers are preoccupied with competitive elimination, and that connoisseurs of excellence will still have to wait a long time for the publication of a collection of "the 100 best games of the year...."

Many years ago, Levidov, in his book referred to earlier, asserted that it is out of the combination of sport and art,

> "the one combination in the whole of human practice, demanding a testing of creative strength, repeated constant testing, and only through events namely of a competitive nature—that the tragedy of chess arises, the equal of which, of course, is not known either by people in sport, or by people in art".

This is a deep conception. Chess is cruel when its competitive mechanism is insufficiently sensibly controlled. Levidov wrote his lines, meditating on the ageing Steinitz. And today, goodness knows, the reflections of defeats by players of the older generation take on dramatic shades, while the eternal mercilessness of youth in present-day chess is intensified one hundred-fold by the procedure of competitive elimination and the system of individual coefficients. The fate of a chess player today is counted by history in units of rating, in the coefficients of Professor Élő.

Without a doubt, the introduction of a system of individual coefficients has reinforced the "status" of modern chess as a sport, in which achievements are measured objectively in points. Is this a good thing? Is this a progressive system? It all depends on your point of reckoning.

> "...Chess possesses a rare virtue—an objective method of comparing successes. The result of an event—the sum total of wins, draws and losses—gives an idea of the effectiveness of a player's performance, whereas in many other fields of mental activity (science, literature) there is an absence of exact criteria. It should be added that the

numerical performances characterizing a player's play enable one to compare not only the successes and capabilities of various people, but to record consistently and accurately the talent of an individual player over the whole of his career."

Thus wrote Nikolai Krogius in an article published in 1972 in the newspaper *64*. Here is formulated a definite viewpoint, which one can dispute or with which one can agree. From our point of view, this position, which is by no means supported on scientific grounds, is an undoubted reflection of the modern process of dragging chess into the sphere of numerical sport. (Incidentally, this process has already received something of a public blessing. Even leading newspapers print the results of a tournament in the form of a table, which in no way differs from that of a football championship.)

Today, a genuine cult of individual coefficients is developing. One frequently comes across masters who reckon up their coefficient before every game. Vlastimil Hort remarks that he saw how, in a junior tournament, players would not turn up for a round if in that game their Élő coefficient could only go down, and to increase it was impossible, and that the purely competitive interest has greatly outstripped the creative. It is no accident that, at the start of the 42nd USSR Championship, Lyev Polugayevsky complained: "What a terrible tournament, the average coefficient in it is so low!" Well, one can understand him, since a high rating has become an unusual guarantee of obtaining a place in a "good" tournament. Besides, as the French proverb says: "Everyone is satisfied with his mind, but dissatisfied with his position...."

Ratings are criticized, but mainly because of imperfections in the system of calculation: "...at times the objective picture [this is a commentary on the list of players, the FIDE rating list, published in 1974 in *64—the authors*] here is distorted. A player who is successful on one occasion can remain for a long time among the best, thanks to his once only 'acquired capital' ...." "...the range of Soviet tournaments covered by the Élő system is still too narrow, which reflects on the coefficients of our developing masters."

What is there to add here? This is criticism from the position of a "numerical" sport.

And so there is the problem of supporting one's "arithmetic reputation", as Mikhail Tal once expressed it. He promptly added: "Arithmetic is one thing, chess is another" (in an interview for the newspaper *64* after his victory in the 42nd USSR Championship). We can merely express our solidarity with Tal. To reconcile, to coordinate the "points" problem with problems of creativity is by no means simple. Bent Larsen, for example, did not succeed in doing this, when he declined to participate in the 21st Olympiad, for the reason that results in team events reflect on individual coefficients. Larsen's refusal is an action of an individual character. Much more dangerous is the shift in public chess consciousness in the direction of "points" chess, a shift which is obviously one of the main sources of present-day chess pragmatism.

When in 1966 Professor Árpád Élő suggested introducing a system of coefficients, he argued his proposal and produced an amusing graph, a kind of "lives in ratings". A glance at it (Fig. 1) can give a clear impression of the "mutual relations" at high level in a historical perspective. Of course, this is interesting, and, moreover, not so much amusing as dramatic. In general, it would be not at all a bad thing if the Élő system had remained an auxiliary instrument of historical research, and had not entered into the life of chess as an instrument of its present-day competitive organization. (It is interesting, for example, to calculate, as was recently done by Sir Richard Clarke in *The British Chess Magazine* (March, April and May 1973) that out of the twenty-five strongest players from Steinitz to Fischer, Emanuel Lasker came out in first place. Or to re-check, for example, the calculations of Sonnenborne, who, back in 1890, made Steinitz the leader from 1867 to 1889 by a simple averaging of points and percentages.)

The introduction of the system of individual coefficients has done much to promote the emergence of a whole generation of chess fighters, players "without prejudices", preaching chess realism. Their aims are crystal-clear—the attainment of victory. Their chess banner is rationalism. They resort to risk only in extreme cases, and prefer to play "correct chess". They are physically fit, and are prepared to wage a protracted, tiring, unattractive struggle, striving to decide its outcome by technical means.

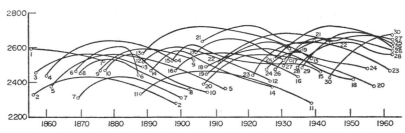

Fig. 1. The "lives in ratings" of great chess players

1. Anderssen	7. Schallopp	13. Lasker	19. Nimzowitsch	25. Botvinnik
2. Bird	8. Mason	14. Janowski	20. Tartakover	26. Reshevsky
3. Paulsen	9. Chigorin	15. Maróczy	21. Capablanca	27. Keres
4. Steinitz	10. Gunsberg	16. Marshall	22. Alekhine	28. Najdorf
5. Blackburne	11. Mieses	17. Rubinstein	23. Euwe	29. Smyslov
6. Zukertort	12. Tarrasch	18. Vidmar	24. Kashdan	30. Petrosian

It would seem that the emergence into the world arena of this detachment of rationalistic fighters poses anew the old problems of the chess press, problems, the sources of which are not difficult to follow in chess history, which is full of the struggle between representatives of the romantic and the rationalistic tendencies. Also appearing in a new light now are the problems of the interpretation of moral and aesthetic values in chess, as is the role of chess in spiritual culture.

Some 50 years ago, Richard Reti, analysing the results of the Capablanca–Alekhine match, wrote that "only out of those players who take account of the slightest disadvantages of a position, and avoid meaningless risk, do genuine masters develop", and that when "from masters 'sharp play' is demanded, what is often meant by these fine words is simply bad play." Reti was attempting to justify the World Champions in front of the general public, in front of those who are now called "the chess community", and attempted to vindicate them by the fact that "in their extreme caution they displayed their mastery to the highest degree." And, as though sensing a certain portion of guilt for the "extreme caution of Alekhine and Capablanca", Reti promptly explained Alekhine's victory as being due to his style, "full of fantasy". It has to be said that public "pressure" made itself known even in those distant times.

To judge from certain articles by chess journalists, the public has remained as it was before. The effusive E. Ilyin, who regularly writes in verse about chess, criticizes the creators of the drawing atmosphere at the USSR Championship First League in 1979, and suggests "taking penalties" in chess. Harry Golombek in the London *Times* writes that, for the participants in the Wijk aan Zee tournament, "play was obviously not a creative act, but an enforced labour, otherwise they would not have agreed draws after the 14th, 13th or even the 11th move.... Had I been one of the spectators I would have taken along to the session a book of Tal's games, so as not to fall asleep through boredom."

However, serious discussions about the creative content of games, about romanticism and fantasy, occur, alas, more and more rarely. As it is, everything is clear—chess players need points and places. And success nowadays is achieved simply: "When Taimanov offered me a draw, and I had little time remaining, I agreed without hesitation. My position, it is true, was rather better, but taking all the circumstances into account...." This is from an interview with Aleksandr Belyavsky, on becoming one of the winners of the 42nd USSR Championship. "I have become more rational as a player," he declared almost with pride.

The rational style is present-day reality. The founder of this style can probably be considered to be Fischer. He worked out, and brought into practice, a new style in the struggle for chess points. His play differed sharply from that of players from the older generation in its efficiency, vigour, amazing straight-forwardness, and in his fanatical belief in his own chess qualities. This combination was not to be found in the arsenal of his predecessors. The Champions of previous decades basically regarded themselves as people of a creative nature, and endeavoured by their play to enrich the treasury of chess thought. These grandmasters, although they battled with one another for points, nevertheless regarded as of paramount importance the achievement of a high creative standard, and from individual instances tried to draw general conclusions. However, being captivated by the aesthetics of the game, they all to a man underestimated the competitive aspect of the chess struggle.

In the 1960s Fischer took much from the creative arsenal of the Champions of previous years, in the main that which links chess with sport, namely, an ideal daily routine, maximum capacity for work in training periods, instant replies in clear positions, and an avoidance of thorny problems in practical play. And at the same time, day after day of analysis of these same positions in the quiet of his study, a thorough examination right to the endgame of the main opening systems, and a rational utilization of chess time.

But this is, so to speak, an explanation of chess "from within". The present-day rationalistic world outlook on chess has a social basis which is considerably broader than in, say, the forties and fifties. This is big-time sport, with its prolific, continuous system of elimination, and also its other extreme—the multi-million army of sports fans. And it has to be said that this dynamic pragmatism of big-time sport is in keeping with the modern style of life in general. Direct, purposeful, dynamic activity without prejudices. Professionalism, without its aggravating doubts and complexes. A utilitarian view of life. Daniil Granin related that, after the publication of his booklet about A. A. Lyubishchev, *Eta Strannaya Zhizn* [This Strange Life], he was bombarded with letters from engineers who, to economize on time, wanted to utilize immediately the system of recording spent time conceived by the deep creative personality of Lyubishchev. Such an approach is not simply fashionable, but to some extent reflects certain processes of cultural development in the era of the scientific-technological revolution.

How should one regard this? Of course, there are various ways. It seems to us that rationalism leads to a lack of spiritual independence, and threatens the loss of creative potential, specially when it is a question of art. Here it is so easy to end up in the position of certain of Konenkov's compatriots, who, discussing his sculpture *The Stone Cutter*, suggested that "it is made in Moscow out of cast iron, springs are attached, and a machine is obtained which will itself smash stones."

Utilitarianism also creates a new public, a "lighter" version of it. Nowadays, people with a different aesthetic experience are coming "into chess". Their co-anxiety with the action on the stage relates to the result, rather than the process. The thoughts and feelings of the sports fan are spreading to chess to the same extent as in other types of sport. And the responsibility for this is borne, of course, by the new "points" style. It would appear that here there is a vicious circle. The style, manner and attitude to the game are formed by amateur enthusiasts. The latter raise up their sports heroes, their idols. Abroad, Fischer in his time played the role of an "intellectual superstar", something of a James Bond in chess. Present-day sports heroes are not especially concerned with the fate of chess art, and by that new impoverished conception of chess which is formed in mass recognition. This is the impoverished conception of chess only as a sport, detached from traditional chess culture, from a game full of aesthetic content. "But I wish once again to remind you that in chess everything is decided by points, and in the end we urge on theory by practice' "—thus did Vladimir Tukmakov conclude his article "Play without prejudices", published in the August 1974 issue of *Yunost* [Youth].

The present-day chess fan is just as intransigent and fastidious as any other. A defeated champion withdraws into the background. Now he is already in the second, and then the third top ten in the rating list. He has lost a part of his professional value. A few more years, and he is already a veteran. Of course, he is a respected person, and he can write about chess, and give lectures to fans. But he is already outside the competitive carousel, his place has been taken by someone else, and perhaps the only things that remain for him are his best games, won or lost.... But why do these remain only for him?

Viktor Vasiliev has found some splendid, sincere words about the actors on the chess stage (cf. *Teatr*, **8,** 1974). Chess is indeed a spectacle, where the spectators share anxiety and experience pleasure. Without the association of spectators with chess art, a game of chess is transformed into an emptiness, a mediocre sports competition. The public must be present at the time when "something is happening" on the stage, remarks Bent Larsen. But now what happens is something different, and instead of a grateful public, valuing creativity, art and mastery, in the audience are sports fans, many of whom simply wait for the result, a ready-made decision, while discussing with their neighbour the state of the tournament table.

We have consciously laid it on thick, and are prepared to apologize to chess fans and enthusiasts. But we would sincerely wish to pass on the feeling, which is constantly with us, of chagrin and disappointment: numerical rationalism is strangling the entertainment aspect and artistry, without which chess cannot live.

The problem of man in big-time sport is, of course, a thousand times more diverse and complex than it appears in our subjective comments. Besides, we have looked at things from the special, foreshortened viewpoint of chess. But here, perhaps more strikingly than anywhere else, general tendencies, provoking suspicion, have become apparent. The pragmatic approach, the desire for points (or half-points)—this is far from that ideal, far from those social and moral values which, multiplying a thousand times, are constantly generated in the wonderful world of chess.

Take the situation of big events, let's say, for instance, the elimination matches for the World Championship. Before a match the press actively discusses the question: who will win? During the match—what chances does so-and-so have? After the match—yes, the winner was the one who was stronger, more competitive and courageous, the one who displayed the greater endurance, will-to-win, etc. The television camera, casting its eye over the tables or demonstration boards, brings the spectator to the field of battle, and a mass of people are plunged into the atmosphere of the event, they absorb it, become excited, respond to the results in shades of patriotic or pseudo-patriotic feeling, split themselves into two camps—I am for the one, he is for the other.... This is the world of big-time sport with its idols and fans, with its emotions of victory and defeat!

And chess? Merely a background on which the battle develops. But possibly this is another form of chess, which has broken away from traditional chess culture, from the intellectual game, full of aesthetic content and maintaining that high creative potential, so necessary to man?

CHAPTER 2.

Homo Ludens

QUESTIONS of cultural, progressively-moral education, and of the harmonious development of personality, its spiritual physical capabilities, are highly important in the entire realm of the communistic education of the workers. Our socialist way of life is based upon a close combination of culture and leisure, introducing the mass of the people to the heights of man's cultural heritage, in the organization of leisure which to the greatest degree answers this noble question.

The cultural potential of an individual is not only his realizable spiritual and physical capabilities, it is the intellectual and emotional, ideological and moral possessions with which each one of us starts off in life, in work and in leisure. Spare time in socialist society is becoming more and more a function of "the complete development of the individual". It is "both leisure, as well as time for more elevated activity" (Marx), for the direct and free creation of cultural values, the user of which is the creator himself.

The fact that chess is one form of "elevated activity", was not doubted at all by the organizers of the cultural revolution in the 1930s. Here, with unfeigned enthusiasm, is what was written by N. V. Krylenko:

"As an instrument of culture, and as a powerful means of cultivating the best qualities of a person, and as a means of developing the aesthetic, intellectual, artistic and volitional qualities in him, chess is such a powerful means of cultural education and re-education, that it can be ignored or underestimated only by ignorant or narrow-minded people, who are incapable of understanding either the

15

whole diversity of life, or, in particular, the many-sided nature of human creativity."

In those now distant years chess was rightly valued as an instrument of cultural struggle, as a key factor in the cultural revolution. Today we will perhaps smile, on learning that 60% of the "proletarian bench staff" played chess, and that this was judged a major achievement. History remembers the slogan, "Not a single village library, in which there is no recreation and reading room, and so that in every recreation and reading room there are chess and draughts sets." The public chess organizer was one of the central figures in the physical culture movement at that time. One is filled with a feeling of pride today when one picks up a small grey leaflet with the heading in large letters: "The Tatar Chess and Draughts Player". The issue of 13th March 1932 reports on the ceremonial opening in the House of Unions of the All-Union Chess Competitions, and emphasizes that these competitions "are aimed not at the qualified chess player, but at the public chess organizer—the creator of socialist construction." The editorial comment is touching: "The irregular appearance of our newspaper is explained by a shortage of paper. The editorial board will take all possible measures to regularize the publication of the newspaper...."

At that time chess was of course "assimilated" in the unified physical culture movement of the country. But the leaders of organizations in the 1930s perspicaciously were aware of the still very weak roots of that social phenomenon known nowadays as big-time sport, and gave it an openly negative assessment. Thus, in a resolution at the 7th All-Union Chess and Draughts Convention (Moscow, October 1931), it was established that "aspiring to raise one's qualification, i.e. qualitative level of play, has nothing in common with harmful phenomena, such as the pursuit of points, etc., which are an expression of a narrowly individual approach to chess."

Today it would be absurd to share this position completely, and we value the striving towards gaining high competitive titles as a powerful stimulus for the mass development of sport, and of physical and spiritual culture. But another point of the resolution from this convention definitely appeals to us:

"The Convention observes that the currently operating system, of determining the results of events by the counting of points, has a number of defects, since, on the one hand, little account is taken of individual creativity, while, on the other hand, the system of reckoning (one, half, nought) is too crude for determining the authentic results of certain games.... The Convention suggests that a study be made of the question of making a more precise reckoning of a game by means of a differentiated evaluation not only of its final position (mate, stalemate, etc.), but also its internal content, giving an impression of the creative level of individual chess and draughts players."

Well now, in our day these questions are no nearer to being solved, a fact which we regret (however, one of the authors has frequently raised the idea of a differentiated evaluation, and... has been labelled a dreamer).

As a factor of cultural life, spiritual development and the organization of leisure, chess is practically passed over by social science, for no apparent reason. The works of the 1930s did not, and indeed could not, contain a scientific analysis or statistical material. But it is an amazing fact that, in our day, sociologists do not recognize chess. Possibly there are difficulties in defining the status of chess within the structure of "the leisure use of culture". But this is no excuse, especially when we have excellent sociological studies of spare time, such as the works by Grushin, Gordon and Klopov. Indeed, in the interesting book by the latter two authors, *Chelovek Posle Raboty* (Man after Work), 1972, we were unable to find chess in any one of the three spheres where one might have expected to: 1. non-professional creativity of cultural values and amateur work (pursuits); 2. non-professional games (dominoes, lotto, cards); 3. physical culture and sport. In a questionnaire attached to the book by B. A. Grushin, *Svobodnoye Vremya* (Free Time), 1967, chess came 20th (out of 30) in spare-time activities, in the section "other collective games (draughts, chess, dominoes)", between "card-playing" and "visiting restaurants, bars and cafes".

We do not know how chess should be categorized in the structure of leisure, but we are convinced that its high cultural and creative significance as "an elevated activity" should be reflected in sociological studies.

There are many forms of cultural links outside the family. Perhaps chess is close to these forms. Or perhaps chess should be differentiated into competitive, recreational, social, family, and so on. At any rate, work is needed here. Otherwise we will have to be satisfied with the sociological cognition of chess, as depicted by one of Shushkin's heroes:

> "You should also learn to play chess, Slavka. Suppose you find yourself in some group of people: some will want to drink, others will be up to various tricks, but you can ask about chess: "Does anyone want to play?" They immediately have a different attitude to you...."

A sociological analysis of chess is necessary, first and foremost, because chess is one of the most universal and democratic phenomena of cultural life. Although the present growth of interest in chess has been brought about by the powerful stimulus of competitive interest (particularly meaningful, of course, is the fact that the prize fund for those disputing the World Championship has been raised to $5 million), the participation itself of millions in chess deserves the attention of sociologists. According to data of the USSR Central Chess Club, we have in our country 4 million organized, i.e. registered, chess players, participating in events and attending chess circles and clubs. However, the number of people who come into contact with chess, who read about chess, and with some degree of activity or other discuss the events of the chess world, is probably an order of magnitude larger. This gigantic number is explained, it seems to us, by the amazing democracy of chess, a mechanism which draws together the "rank and file" enthusiast with the top personalities, illuminated by the rays of public attention and interest, who are, first and foremost, outstanding sportsmen.

This mechanism of rapprochement, of "levelling", may seem illusory, but it is hard to disclaim it as an opportunity for self-improvement, the development of the chess ability of an individual, and perhaps of certain qualities of character—at the expense of the work, talent and knowledge of another person. The manifestation of this phenomenon, which is for the most part not realized, is readily traced by analysing letters to newspaper editors, to the Central Chess Club, and to grandmasters.

Some write, so to speak, in search of truth. "Forgive me if I am wrong"—this is the leitmotif of these letters, "but you, grandmaster, write that after 28 R×f7 it is hardly possible for White to win. But in another newspaper, another grandmaster writes that 28 R×f7 would have settled the outcome immediately. Whom should I believe?" There are also letters of this sort: "I should like the editor to explain to me, as closely as possible after the example of Chigorin, how White is supposed to win after 42... Re7-d7. With regards." Comrade N., a correspondence player from Leningrad, makes a direct appeal to a grandmaster: "I have a big favour to ask of you: analyse this ending for me, and send me your reply." A certain K. from Moscow asks: "In one of our tournament games the following position was reached.... Can White, to move, draw? Please excuse any inconvenience, yours sincerely...."

Others contemplate. Comrade L. sends to a grandmaster a graph of three games from the Spassky–Fischer match, where along the abscissa he has plotted the move number, and along the ordinate—the potential of the position. "The method is, of course, incomplete, and needs to be improved, but perhaps it is of interest to you, grandmaster?" A third group gives advice with the spirit of the true supporter: "You must not even think about a draw. You yourself must understand perfectly well that in the last few games Botvinnik has not been Botvinnik...." This letter, of course, is dated 1951.... There are many such letters in the archives of every grandmaster.

Here we see the lively, creative, mass interest in chess, and at the same time a reflection of its democratic spirit as an instrument of intellectual and emotional contact. Obviously this interest has deep social and psychological sources.

The ability to serve the spiritual improvement of an individual determines the high social significance of chess, and its educational function. Self-discipline, independence of thinking, and a sense of responsibility—these are perhaps the main traits which chess gives to those who take it seriously. Bent Larsen is correct in emphasizing the happy combination in chess of a whole series of splendid qualities: "will-to-win, self-control, sense of logic, sense of psychology, good disposition, fantasy, ability to make lengthy calculations, and ability to concentrate." Emanuel Lasker also expressed it wonderfully well:

"Anyone who wishes to cultivate in himself the ability to think independently in chess must avoid all that is dead in it: made-up theories, which are based on very few examples and on an enormous amount of fabrication; the habit of playing against weaker opponents; the habit of avoiding danger; the habit of imitating uncritically, and, without due thought, repeating variations and rules employed by others; self-satisfied vanity; unwillingness to admit one's own mistakes..."

Isn't it possible to apply these words to the entire spiritual activity of man?

Without a doubt, as a systematic pursuit, chess aids the development of a critical mind, of objectivity and self-criticism.

"By means of chess I developed my character. Chess teaches you first and foremost to be objective. In chess you can become a great master only by recognizing your mistakes and deficiencies. Just the same as in life,"

wrote Alexander Alekhine. Even today these words still hold true. After all, the aspects of intellect which are translated into reality in chess are in particular those which are dependent upon its purposefulness and its practical character. Something which applies fully to chess is the demand of "unity of mind and will", embodied, as the Soviet sociologist B. M. Teplov wrote, in the activity of a military leader. And it is only as an additional trait that one should regard the assertion by the well-known English chess master, diplomat and businessman Alexander, that chess "cultivates management ability".

Perhaps even more important is the fact that chess can serve as a highly valuable source of great creative achievements.

About this, unfortunately, little is said, perhaps for the reason that in the general formulation of the question, the nature and the sense of creative achievements in chess have been far from clarified. A curious error in the evaluation of the creative potential of chess was made by such a perspicacious person as Lewis Carroll. He wrote:

"Intellectual diversions are necessary for our spiritual health. Among such diversions one can undoubtedly number games like backgammon, chess and the new game of "Halla". Without becoming a first-

class player in any of these games, you cannot extract from it anything which could be *regarded as a result* [our italics—*the authors*].
While you are playing, the process of the game and victory afford
you satisfaction, but you do not gain any result which you can
value or use in any way."

Carroll can readily be excused. He could not have foreseen that out of
a modest "intellectual diversion" for a few would grow a powerful
branch of mass leisure, and that it was this game, and not backgammon,
that would serve as a training ground for the testing of characters and
feelings, and would emerge as a unique model of the manifestation of
the highly creative mind.

   The Dutch philosopher Heisinga has written a book entitled *Homo
Ludens* (Man at Play). From a large amount of historical cultural material, Heisinga shows that competitive play is the precursor of creative
activity, a manifestation of "the gain of the creator", "the free disclosing
of a person's creative strengths", be he a scientist, a virtuoso performer,
or a sportsman. In the conventional playing world a person can realize
his creative potential, which is by no means always possible in real life.
Play is always a palliative of activity, but activity that is creative. Similar
ideas, although coloured with deep pessimism, were expressed about the
motives of creativity by Albert Einstein. By strength of creative imagination, a person aims to

   "create in himself a simple and clear picture of the world, so as to get
   away from the world of feelings, so as to a certain extent to attempt
   to replace this world by the picture so created. This is done by the
   artist, the poet, the theorizing philosopher and the natural scientist,
   each in his own way. Into this picture and its formulation, man trans-
   fers the centre of gravity of his spiritual life, so as to find in it calm
   and confidence, which he is unable to find in the over-crowded,
   dizzy rotation of his own life."

   In any game, man, by force of imagination, in the words of Aldous
Huxley,

   "is transported into a strictly regulated world, created by himself,
   where everything is clear, sensible and capable of being understood.
   The spirit of competition, added to the intrinsic charm of the game,

makes it even more fascinating, while the thirst for victory and the poison of vanity lend a particular sharpness to the game...."

In chess, imagination not only transports a person into a different, conventional world of play, but is also substantiated in the very movements of the chess pieces, completing one's ideas. Those pictures which pass before the mental vision of the player are the product of imagination and thought, and it is a pity that we see only the final trace of this work, by following the demonstration board or reading through the score of a chess game.

The relative interconnection between the real world and the world of play in the activity of people has been poorly studied. It has perhaps been best expressed by A. Bezimensky:

"Yes, this is all true, but even so,
But even so I should like to say,
That life is similar to chess,
But to live is not the same as to play chess."

From possibly all games, and in particular from backgammon and bridge (the scheming in which is close to chess), chess is distinguished by one remarkable ability—anyone, be he a master or an enthusiast, can show his worth in it. It is the only game which is accessible to all ages, to everyone. Everyone can put into the game "unbending will, noble emotion, honesty of thinking, and a hatred of opportunism, lack of principle, cowardice and mental and volitional weakness" (Mikhail Levidov). Everyone can give up to chess a part of his soul, a part of his personality. Chess gratefully repays this gift with interest—a person sees himself as a creative individual and gains confidence, even when enveloped, as often happens, by a feeling of deep creative dissatisfaction. And at the same time the high social and ethical destiny of chess, perhaps even self-assertion, imperiously finds its way into our life.

But chess gives more than this. Like any other genuine form of creativity, it gives man hope, mobilizes him, elevates him in his own eyes, and opens before him an intelligent and, under certain conditions, a high moral goal. After all, "who would dare to assert that, in an open and honest duel, truth suffers a defeat?" (John Milton).

A competition with you yourself—this, in the final analysis, is the point of playing chess. It would seem that a competition with yourself has much more significance in life, than has one with an opponent. It is competition with yourself that gives an impetus to your entire emotional life. The proud joy resulting from a realization of your own strength, from a plan fulfilled; the bitter disappointment from an understanding of your own weakness, from the missed opportunities—these are two emotional extremes. These emotions are ingenuous, understandable, and worthy of respect. In one of his letters, Sergey Prokofiev wrote: "But there is one blemish on my well-being: in a simultaneous display I lost to Capablanca, whereas the game was a clear draw. It is enough to make one weep, and all my hopes are on gaining revenge the day after tomorrow." Another time his rejoicing was boundless: "Yesterday I at last defeated Capablanca, playing against him in a simultaneous display," he writes on a postcard with a portrait of Capablanca. "You must agree that this is an extremely remarkable occurrence." And in a letter of 23rd May 1914: "Since the day that I defeated Capablanca, nothing has happened...."

The psychological nature of such feelings still awaits its description. Perhaps the main thing is in that mental, emotional discharge which chess gives with each encounter, each meeting. In his youth, Academician P. L. Kapitsa once remarked to the English master Milner-Barry: "Chess brings the mind into a state of balance." From our own experience we can readily confirm these words. For this same reason chess players love blitz (lightning chess), which gives a rapid and significant discharge. To a certain extent one can agree with one of the first researchers into the game of chess—Professor A. P. Nechayev, who remarked that the basic source of pleasure in the game was "the replacement of a feeling of tension with one of relief or of 'solution'." The psychological impacts of a solved and an unsolved problem are probably very great. We find difficulty in somehow measuring them, and can only guess that, in the system of motivation towards active work, towards creativity, they play a significant role.

There are two further factors which deserve to be discussed within this context. As Emanuel Lasker said, what fascinates us in chess is its pure expediency. It is for this reason that people give themselves up into the power of chess, although, as this thinker remarked: "they only vaguely realize this, rather than clearly acknowledge it." It is insufficient for a man to be successful, he wishes it to be inevitable. It is not enough to solve a problem, it must be solved with the inexorability of logic. This validity, or, if you like, fatality in chess attracts and tempts millions of people. Here, in chess, as Stefan Zweig expressed it, people seek "the beginning and the goal." Here are joined the new and the old, the unusual is linked with the usual, mysteries are conceived and solved, and this process, inexhaustible like the world, is completed with iron inexorability. It is this assimilation of the new with the old, the unknown with the known, the non-obvious with the obvious, which comprises the essence of high intellectual enjoyment.

And finally, about the aesthetic sensation provoked by the solving of a problem. In chess there are ample difficulties, and therefore much beauty. The criteria of beauty, which are deeply individual, manifest themselves in chess as a powerful, abstract and impartial force. Here each has his aesthetics, and at the same time it is unified and sovereign. Everything that appeals to us in a game, be it a combination or a manoeuvre, a trap or a study-like ending, the complex logic of a plan or the geometrical harmony of coordination—all these are distinctive aesthetic "invariants". It is these invariants that we love, we are delighted by them, and we wait for the master to reveal them to us again and again, filling our souls with the happy experience of beauty.

As a game, chess offers a person an accessible form of relaxation, leisure and amusement. Here chess, like a classical comedy, fulfils the function of relaxing, while maintaining in man the strength, ability and aspiration to improve. Thanks to the beauty of its art, chess creates more. It generates a creative frame of mind, and, like a classical tragedy, fulfils the function of inspiration, of striving for the unattainable.

"We, people, are given a piece of the Universe, so that we should get to know it, we try to reach its depths in not just one way, we probe it with our behaviour, science, poetry, love.... We need various methods so as to measure our world with it." Wonderful words by K. Chapek. How good it is that chess, in spite of its arbitrary nature and the crowded state of its 64 squares, gives people a means of measuring their world.

CHAPTER 3.

The Joy of Creativity and the Bitterness of Craftsmanship

THE ART of chess has not yet assumed its place among the other arts. This is easy to see, but not easy to explain. There can be no art—and this includes chess art, of course—without interpretation. For high forms of art, talented interpretation is required. Concepts used in everyday thinking are of little use for interpretation. This is why the interpreters of chess art borrow their vocabulary from the other arts—music, poetry and painting. This is why the authors are fighting the temptation to take up the almost surrealistic musicological terminology of Dmitri Kabalevsky or Svetlana Vinogradovaya.

Emanuel Lasker wrote about chess in deep and passionate terms. This wonderful gift is, alas, one that is not encountered nowadays. What is more, in our era one feels rather shy of openly using a high literary style. If today someone were to write as follows:

"The vocabulary of a chess piece is not as limited as is thought: ambition—in fulfilling its work, fury—if it is prevented from doing this, despair—on account of its undeservedly bitter lot, rejoicing —regarding a happy occurrence, mockery—of the opponent, whose piece has blocked the way, hatred—of anyone who threatens the king, laughter—when it succeeds in avoiding a trap...."

the internal editor, sitting inside each one of us, would promptly make an angry protest. But Lasker raised onto a pedestal the creators of chess art, conquering the routine, killing the stereotyped, seeking the unknown, erring, but—creating. About "players without prejudices" one does not write in this way.

Chess is a fortunate art form. It does not live only in the minds of its witnesses. It is retained in the best games of masters, and does not disappear from the memory when the masters leave the stage. It is always alongside: it cannot be lost and is available to everyone, even if the master himself is lost to the art. It rewards anyone who asks it questions. Its strength is in its interpretation. This phenomenon, inherent in chess, music or painting, enables one repeatedly to reproduce beauty and to afford aesthetic pleasure, frequently deepening and strengthening it by the talent and artistic experience of the interpreter.

Any art can be created only by great masters, wrote Hemingway. This is both correct and incorrect as regards chess. Correct, because only a true artist, a great master, experiences life as a continuous novelty, and, taking everything that has been comprehended and discovered in his art before him, fully armed with knowledge, he goes further, discarding the unnecessary, and creates his own, new art. It is incorrect, because in chess, creativity and art are not hidden behind the stamps of mastery, and the joy of creative success is accessible to anyone. Chess is a sea in which a gnat may drink and an elephant may bathe. So runs the Indian proverb. Quite well, if somewhat crudely, stated. The whole point is that chess is unified in its artistic value, but it is only in the games of the great masters that this aesthetic value is blessed with authority, that it is revealed with masterful interpretation and by this is objectified, and becomes accessible to all. But in millions of amateur games it creeps in imperceptibly, and for ever remains a subjective value "for oneself".

Chess is in the highest degree an individual form of creativity. For this reason, to describe its essence, its constituent components, its harmony or technique, is just as difficult as it is for a composer to describe his work. But, as in music, here it is easy to draw the attention of the average enthusiast. The latter is just as capable of experiencing artistic effect and emotional impact as is a listener at a musical performance. Unfortunately, those who live and work today in big-time chess, as well as the interpreters of their creativity, are inclined to talk mainly about the competitive changes in fortune in games, rather than the artistic components contained in them. And this is not a matter of the intellectual or ethical snobbery of masters, but that they, like everyone else, are subject to the competitive rationalistic spirit of our time. The aesthetic loss suffered by chess as a result of this would appear to be quite considerable.

Perhaps we do too little for the artistic education of chess players. Of course, it is easy to acknowledge that the art of the "old masters" is growing old, but the distance of time gives rise to an immutable scepticism, so characteristic of the twentieth century. But we invariably admire games "in the good old style", despite the fact that the few games of this sort are drowned in a sea of efficient, modern games, played without risk. In recalling striking games (it is a pity that we do this so rarely), we realize that our delight at them is based on a deep aesthetic feeling, distinctive, but in no way differing from the feeling which seizes us in front of a beautiful building, the harmonious beauty of nature, or human physical perfection. This aesthetic feeling, this experience, enriches us.

Genuine art is always the finished article.

"The reason why art can enrich us," remarks Niels Bohr, "lies in its ability to remind us of harmonies which are inaccessible to systematic analysis." Rarely do we realize this. In general, mechanisms of art, based on the perception of harmony, are not always clearly realized. The forming of such a perception requires a special psychological act— "an intimately individual aesthetic experience.... It is for this reason that the results of artistic comprehension of reality do not flow directly into the fund of collective knowledge, i.e. evidence, which has a forced and directly transferable character"—F. V. Bassin, *Problema Bessoznatelnovo* (The Problem of the Unsonscious), Moscow, 1968. This situation is fully characteristic of chess art and of chess knowledge.

We do not know, and cannot see directly, the working of the mechanism which gives rise to a creative idea, but we can judge on it from the result. And the more indisputable the result, the deeper the aesthetic feeling influences us. References to feelings may provoke surprise when it comes to talking about things which are apparently linked only with thinking. But in chess, as in mathematics, there is harmony of form, geometric beauty and expressiveness, and free play of the imagination. And there is a multitude of examples of how the choice of the best plan or move in chess is guided by beauty. A harmonious idea is almost always correct. Without exaggerating greatly, it can be said that it is aesthetic feeling which attunes the intellect towards searching, and leads it there.

The nature of aesthetic feeling meets the deepest demands of man as a product of social-cultural development, and, most probably, as a biological creature. This nature was aptly expressed by the great French anthropologist and structuralist, Claude Levi-Strauss:

"Aesthetic pleasure, composed of a multitude of confusions and respites, of deceptive and excessively rewarded expectations, is the result of a challenge thrown down to us by an artistic production. It is also formed out of a contradictory sensation of the fact that the test, to which the production subjects us, is insuperable, and of the fact that it is ready to give us completely unforesen opportunities to triumph over these tests."

Of course, in chess too the aesthetic feeling arises out of a realization of difficulties overcome as a feeling of happiness, as a reward for waiting, for uneasiness of mind. This gift of nature is impartial, and it lies at the basis of creativity, of any sort—professional or amateur.

In chess, all three components inherent in any creative activity—idea, realization and interaction—are combined in wonderful fashion. An idea, the product of the activity of an intellect, is translated into reality, it is embodied in the concrete visible form of the movement of a piece, it is recorded in the score of a game or on the demonstration board, and finds its addressee, the public, spectators and readers, chess enthusiasts throughout the world, associating and interacting with the creator of the idea. In this triunity lies the optimism of chess creativity, although, of course, there is a whole spectrum of "intermediate" states between creative and non-creative activity, which to evaluate and characterize is not easy. This optimism was aptly expressed by Academician A. Ishlinsky, replying to the question: "Is it worth while putting so much effort into chess?"—"It is worth while, because chess gives a man more than he puts into it."

There are at least four factors which bring about the creative nature of chess, and give rise to a feeling of great creative joy.

The first is obvious, and is that the player himself creates artistic riches. Things which are thought up, created, and established by the person himself have always been, and will always remain, an inexhaustible source of joy.

About the second we will speak in more detail. The point is that genuine joy of creation arises only when the created thing appeals to others, when it can afford pleasure and provide joy to those who heed and suffer together with the creator. "The artist is charged only with a unipolar force," wrote Aleksey Tolstoy, "For the flow of creativity a second pole is vitally necessary—one who gives heed, a fellow-sufferer." In art, as in science, the generation of new ideas and images is assisted not by dry, impersonal information, but by personal contact, by the unlimited diversity of resulting connections, and by human warmth. Chess has its own public. And, evidently, the strength of creative experience is not only directly dependent upon the sensation of its involvement in the creative process, but also upon the realization of the fact that this process is accomplished in the eyes of others.

The impact made by art depends upon the expectation of the spectator. Just as the musician extracts for the public the sounds of a charming melody, so the artistic chess player uses his skill to extract from the material at his disposal the beauty of a chess idea. Without an audience there is no creative intensity. Therefore on a deserted stage, alone with himself, the master loses his creative potential, and his torpid soul becomes the prisoner of countless variations, from which he no longer has the strength to escape.

How little we do for the chess public, for the connoisseurs of chess art. We have no specially adapted playing halls for chess performances (journalists readily describe them thus, but alas, without any justification). Neither do we have any demonstration halls, where qualified experts could give explanations to the public, underlining the beauty of the ideas. We do not record the score of a game alongside the demonstration board, for the benefit of spectators who are unable to arrive at the start of the game. We are unable to utilize the possibility of television for the public (only very recently did they learn to do this for the press). The whole organization of chess events is dictated by competitive, rather than entertainment, interests. This is possibly one of the reasons why modern masters do not feel any pangs of conscience when playing for a quick draw.

The third factor is the mysterious beauty of chess, which is a powerful attractive factor. Chess possesses an intrinsic fascination of mystery, although for some this is a mystery of a high art form, while for others it is merely the riddle of Chinese billiards or a musical automaton. We will talk a little about the beauty of art.

It may seem surprising, but we are able and are accustomed to evaluating the beauty of an idea in chess compositions, but not in practical play. It is true that Francois le Lionnais, the well-known French chess enthusiast, has collected 200 games which have received prizes for brilliancy, and has proposed arranging them according to a "scale of beauty"[1] devised by him. But few know about this. Nowadays, in every tournament, a few games are mentioned for their beauty in general, or (so as to satisfy the different concepts of beauty) for "quality": the "best" game, a "consistently conducted attack", etc. No, we do not propose evaluating every game on criteria of beauty, and rewarding the players, although in every game there are two or three beautiful extracts. We are simply reflecting on the question: just how should the beauty of a practical game be understood?

This is a complex question. Too diverse, mobile, unstable and subjective are the criteria of beauty in a chess game. Too different are the standards of beauty. In order to understand and experience a complicated musical work, a symphony, for example, one must possess not only a good ear, but also a certain aesthetic taste. Our chess tastes, as well as our chess "ears", differ no less than those in the auditorium of a concert hall. In addition, today we like this, tomorrow we like that, and then someone will come up and say: "Give over, that's already been

---

[1] Here in approximate translation are the degrees of this scale: difficulty, liveliness (de vivacité), originality, richness, correctness, degree of concealment (unvisible), and unity of logic.

seen." The difficulty, of course, is in the subjective interpretation of beauty.

Why is the King's Gambit beautiful? This is not easily explained. It is encompassed by the romanticism of the games of the old masters, in it the importance of each move is critical, in it there is a profusion of "focal points", points where the conflict is heightened, and finally, in it there are many beautiful final positions which can easily be reached if the opponent has a poor understanding of this opening. In short, here there is daring and risk. Perhaps it is the manifestation of daring which should be placed at the top of that imaginary scale?

Things are no better in chess composition, but somehow they cope with the subjective nature of evaluating a problem or a study. Moreover, at the present time the instrument of expert assessment enables subjectivism to be overcome, and an acceptable general opinion to be worked out. So what about the idea of introducing an evaluation of each game, based initially on a there-point system: banality—nil, correctness—one point, daring—two, there or more points?

One can think also of other scales. It is possible to evaluate "the strictness, completeness, and strength of logical set-ups," concluding, as Botvinnik writes, "in an interesting game," perhaps "tending towards simplicity" and the absence of "superfluous extraneous effects."

It is important to retain and carry that beauty of chess which arises in "the battle against the obvious, against the truism" (Emanuel Lasker). And Richard Reti spoke splendidly about this:

> "That which basically delights us in chess, for all of us—including the dabbler, whose ideal is a combination with sacrifices, and the expert, who for the most part is delighted by the depth of an idea—is one and the same thing: the triumph of a deep, brilliant idea over dull mediocrity, the victory of the individual over the trivial."

Which are "superfluous extraneous effects", and which are genuine, is not so difficult to work out.

The ability of an artist is that he can see the unusual. Banality is a void which is hostile to beauty. As Francis Bacon asserted: "there is no complete beauty in existence which does not contain a certain portion of strangeness." Logic in chess is the middle school. In the upper school there must also be an ability to do away with logic, there must be daring and fantasy. Mikhail Tal has created a considerable number of absurdities, and thus opened a new page in chess creativity.

Finally, the fourth factor of creativity. This is the deep intellectual pleasure of working in a fantastically varied and flexible medium. It is the joy of testing the strength of an idea, the strength of one's imagination. It is that which, first and foremost, distinguishes a thinking person from a thinking machine. But here, in the kingdom of chess thought, it is not phantoms and illusions that dominate, but ideas which receive a swift and immediate realization. Your life in chess is not enclosed within a "sphere of pure thought", the threads of this life are firmly interwoven with the reality of your life and work. Thought, imagination and fantasy in a gigantic combinatorial field lead you from chaos to order, and the appreciation of the reality of this transition, as well as the very fact of productive work by your own intellect, makes you happy.

This is what we think about chess art, creativity and beauty. But there is also another side to the coin.

Chess is not only high-level creativity. It is also craftsmanship, laborious and obligatory, which often leaves serious scars on one's soul. And this craftsmanship sometimes gives rise to deep disillusionment, the disappointment of doubts and misfortunes. "A man is never called into craftsmanship. He is called on only to fulfil his duty and a difficult task," wrote K. Paustovsky. But modern chess possibly refutes these words more than it confirms them. It frequently forces the master to become a craftsman, and not always, unfortunately, in the good sense of this word.

A chess player is like a doctor; he knows the symptoms of illness and the range of medicines. But in a difficult case, when the symptoms are not recognized, medicine cannot help. Everything that you know, that you are able to do, at the decisive moment breaks down, and your one single mistake leads to a fatal outcome. The magic of the master fails to work. And once again you resign yourself to a difficult and delusive search, you seek new medicines, you hope, you wait, again comes a mistake, and it starts all over again. This dependence of success on a chance inaccuracy, the source of which cannot sometimes even be understood, acts just as depressingly as does the carelessness or forgetfulness of a doctor.

In chess you are left to your own resources, and at the same time you are strictly dependent on someone else. On his knowledge and experience, on how attentive he is, on whether he is in the mood for a fight, and finally, on whether the hour of inspiration has come to him. You have doubts while still at home, you don't know whether you'll be able to guess the opening, you feverishly examine his games, poke about in the reference books, seek, and find nothing. You are vexed, you become nervous, you curse yourself and your helplessness, and later you curse yourself a thousand times, if you lose....

Well, and if you know a lot, you anticipate how the game will go, but you are simply not in the mood, and today you have other things on your mind, you arrive at the hall and quickly, masterfully play a dull draw. You do it, and then, when you need it, you do it easily, because you "caught" the opening, because for days and even months you have been preparing, but now you have had to give up all this, immediately, to no purpose, without that striking and deserved result which your labours should have given you.

You three or four good, perhaps even beautiful, games in the tournament—these are the fruits of painstaking, routine, and by no means creative, labour. Three games—you are lucky: grandmaster N had 13 draws altogether, and his labour, which was no less than yours, gave him 50% of the points.

You are composed and steadfast, your head is clear, you like the public, you are generous and wish to bestow upon them your skill, your mental enthusiasm is unusually joyful. But you encounter a force which you had not expected, intuition tells you that just now you are going to be "caught", you yourself don't know this, you haven't seen this, you have passed it by. And you avoid the tempting, beautiful, but dangerous path. You, the master, the servant of art, have forgotten your obligations, you have played a run-of-the-mill game, because you must not take a risk, you must not lose....

This dramatic situation gives rise to many problems. The master spends many long hours alone at the board. He may find a plan, a variation, a move which no-one before him has conceived. Later in the theoretical reference book they will write: a variation or move first employed by so-and-so. Even if someone else has found the same, he does not know this, he is the discoverer, at any rate for himself. Is the master worthy of being called a creator? Is this monotonous, painstaking analysis of opening positions a work which is creative, a contribution to chess art? It is difficult to give a straightforward answer.

Chess theory today is a mass creation by thousands of masters. It is conceived primarily in the quiet of their studies, in private, without any spectators, without the sharpness of creative feeling. It is difficult to say definitely, but this would seem to be a plausible form of creativity. And the funny thing is that this variation found at home can then "cut through" into a brilliantly spectacular attack, which will be applauded by the public and the press. The creative potential of a master is not automatic, but depends to a great extent on his accomplishments and on his opening preparation. Most probably, like the creative potential of a scientist, it is founded on his knowledge. But this constraint due to ignorance (and sometimes even due to knowledge), the feeling of its dependence on the quality of your preparation, the far from simple connection between your creative possibilities and routine preparatory work, often serves as a source of unhappy thoughts, and, possibly, of one of the most bitter of feelings—the loss of independence.

It is unlikely that anyone would dispute the fact that no-one can be creative at a given time, and in a given frame of mind. This is not demanded of a composer, a physicist or a poet. There is no automatic creativity. But there is the automatism of craftsmanship, the ordinary professional solution to a problem. Here, possibly the only way of retaining your creative potential is to have a clear realization of the level and nature of your "automatic" creativity. It is by no means everyone, however, who is capable of such introspection.

Felix Krivine optimistically remarked that "a genuine mountain not only gives birth to a mouse, but also helps it to climb up onto the summit." In chess it is by no means every mouse which succeeds in climbing to the summit of creativity, despite the mountain of work expended. However, this is the case not only, of course, in chess....

Finally, when a creative solution is discovered and translated into reality, interpreted and carried to the public, it appears simple and accessible, the mystery has evaporated from it. The discovery is in a certain sense devalued. It has already nullified the energy of the search. The motive has been realized in the result. This situation in chess is analogous to that in scientific and artistic creativity. But this solution remains for the creator his feat, his achievement. Like everything on this earth, this feat, this accomplishment will be forgotten. And then comes the disappointment and bitterness of loss.

The heavy stamp of craftsmanship, of course, distorts, lowers and sometimes replaces the high spirit of chess creativity and art. But this essentially sad factor cannot and should not serve as a justification for chess pragmatism. It is difficult to agree with grandmaster Suetin, who, in summing up the 42nd USSR Championship, wrote: "Healthy rationalism at the present time is a fashionable creative infection." It is our deep conviction that in chess there can be no healthy rationalism, and certainly not creative!

Justification for the rationalistic spirit did not begin recently.

"Often a great player is forced to be content with an uninteresting draw, if the opponent's play does not give him the opportunity to display his talent. Indeed, the public is not altogether correct in attributing to book theory the blame for the (apparent!) impoverishment of the game of chess."

These words belong to Rudolph Spielmann, a player of sharp combinational talent. He is also alluding to the twentieth century, although these lines were written in the twenties.

Commenting on the match he won against Spassky in 1966, Petrosian wrote: "Can it be expected in such an exceptionally nervy atmosphere, when the strings are stretched to the limit, that the contestants should sacrifice competitive considerations for the sake of creative ones?" Here it is not theory which is to blame, but the nervy atmosphere. The number of such justifications can be multiplied. The authors of such justifications are correct from all points of view, except one—that of chess art, and it is with pleasure that we recall the words of Alekhine:

"The very idea of composition is deeply attractive to me. I would be happy to create all alone.... Oh, that opponent, that partner who is linked to you!.... How much disillusionment does he cause the true artist in chess matters, striving not just for victory, but first and foremost for the creation of a work of art, which has some real value"

although we also appreciate their naïve pathos—after all, a chess game is of necessity the creation of both players. Nevertheless, we fail to find amusing the unusual action of grandmaster Gufeld, who, annotating one of his games, attached to a poor move by his opponent both an exclamation mark and a question mark, the exclamation mark in gratitude to him for his "co-authorship in the creation of an attractive little finish."

CHAPTER 4.

Decisions, Images and Rhythms

"EVERYONE knows how difficult it is to study science and art by a generally accepted system," Jonathan Swift once lamented. Alas, when there is no generally accepted system it is many times more difficult to do this. Modern chess researchers do not, as a rule, talk about a system. They are convinced that chess is a model of intellectual activity, very convenient for laboratory study and experiment, a model of decision taking, so that any system is good, provided that it promises at least some progress.

"This game is a good model for applying the theory of decision-taking... for working out methods of decision-taking in situations where it is impossible to evaluate exactly their consequences," writes Academician V. A. Trapeznikov. In the projected work of the USSR Academy of Sciences Institute of Control Problems is the study of such model problems with the aim of "expanding and deepening understanding of the creative process itself."

Strictly speaking, the more or less systematic study of chess as a model of thinking processes began in the late nineteen fifties in the course of work on heuristic programming. Today in scientific abstract journals, such works are published in the sections "Artificial intelligence", "Decision-taking" and "Problem-solving", along with machine evidence of the theory and recognition of images. This is perfectly logical, and it is quite possible that successes in the creation of artificial intelligence will come to us from an understanding of a chess player's creative thinking.

The model approach, cybernetic conceptual schemes, have also attracted professional psychologists, especially those who love chess. Two Doctors of Psychological Science, V. N. Pushkin and O. K. Tikhomirov, have made a number of attempts to describe the thinking processes of chess players, using highly modern methods such as recording eye movements, and others. But these respected authors have essentially not gone beyond the bounds of the informational-heuristic direction. We should mention, incidentally, that the strictly psychological study of chess would appear to have ended with the unpublished dissertation by B. M. Blumenfeld in 1946; the work by N. V. Krogius, devoted to the psychological preparation of a chess player, is much closer to the psychology of sport than to the psychological study of a chess player's thinking.

The cybernetic plan for studying chess, which at present is undoubtedly a dominant scientific trend, is to a certain extent a reflection of that same "spirit of the times", which has elevated rationalism into a conviction. We have no wish at all to gain the reputation for being reactionaries, incapable of understanding the modern "scientific-rationalistic" world outlook. But isn't too much being left overboard, when arguments come to the fore regarding "abstract", mathematically-analysed chess, about the "working technique of a player" and "rationalisation of thinking"? And yet it is precisely about this that Doctor of Physical and Mathematical Sciences V. Gurary openly writes. "In the future," this author openly asserts, "it will become highly common to regard the chess activity of a certain player as an individual, 'portable' laboratory *for the processing of rational schemes of thinking and behaviour for the arbitrary aims of the entire vital work practice of man*" [our italics — *the authors*]. Such a rationalized future is a cheerless prospect. We will console ourselves, however, with the apt remark by Anatole France: "Science is infallible, but scientists are constantly making mistakes."

Once upon a time the hero of a story was granted three wishes. Modern rationalists in science and in life have surmised that it is perfectly possible to be satisfied with one—to wish that all one's wishes should come true. They strive to solve any problem, and to do this in the most efficient way. But they have ceased to formulate unattainable goals, to which one can only constantly approach. They have paid no attention to ideals. The moral losses from global rationalism are by no means inconsiderable. From this point of view, we see the value of chess as a model of activity, not so much in that it is a convenient means of studying control problems and their rational solution, but rather that it can (and should) serve as a model of a perpetual, undying movement of man towards an ideal, a striving for the wonderful, a model for gaining ever new heights of creative spirit.

Just what are the psychological aspects of decision-taking?

What do psychologists talk about, when they refer to chess?

First and foremost, they talk of the complexity of decision-taking processes. It is mentioned, in particular, that the memory is frequently overloaded with alternatives, that the criteria for comparing alternatives are not given in any clear form, and that uncontrollable factors always come into play. The American researchers Norman and Lindsey write:

"It should not come as a surprise that the mere complexity of decision-taking often leads to the fact that the person despairs, loses heart, and endeavours to delay the choice for as long as possible; in the end, he takes a decision under the pressure of circumstances, without even attempting to imagine to himself all the consequences of this decision. Later, when this has all happened and it is impossible to change anything, there comes the time for suffering and repenting, surmising as to whether or not another, better solution could have been chosen."

Ambrose Bierce's Satan expressed this same thought much more briefly: "Taking a decision means reconciling oneself to the superiority of certain external influences over others."

The limited nature of the methods of studying decisions is perfectly commensurate with the complexity of the problem. Lindsey and Norman correctly point out that people often describe their behaviour as clear and consistent, even if it is not in fact so. In decisions after the event, actual and imaginary actions are always interwoven. The researcher cannot know all the variables, all the factors describing the situation. Psychological components, such as boredom, emotional tension or fatigue sometimes exert a critical influence on decision-taking. In general, the inner world of a person in all its multi-coloured diversity determines not only the choice (and a decision is always an act of choice), but also the very functioning of the choice mechanism. Chess could, evidently, become a model for studying the inner world of a person and his psychological mechanisms. However, psychology does not yet have in its arsenal methods of working with such types of models.

Of course, things have changed since the time of Binet, who wrote in 1894:

„If we were able to look inside the head of a chess player, we would see there a whole world of sensations, images, ideas, emotions and passions, an endless ferment of states of consciousness, in comparison with which all our most painstaking descriptions are merely crude schemes."

Today the descriptions of certain mental processes are highly plausible, and touch on subtle mechanisms. Nevertheless, the majority of results relate to one section, which is logical, rather than psychological—to the representation of the decision process as the mental evaluation of the results of a mental experiment. Claude Shannon wrote about these representations, that "this is an almost exact description of how a computer, playing chess, operates, if the word 'mentally' is replaced by the words 'inside the computer'." Internal, "machine" models, describing "mental experiments" are normally subdivided by psychologists into "interpretive" and "prognostic". The first of these fulfil the function of processing and evaluating the information available, and the second— the construction of a plan and determination of the probable consequences of various decisions. Nowadays it has become customary to load these models with ever more complex functions, and on block-diagrams to draw more and more squares and connections, providing "optimal" plans and decisions. Without denying the certain usefulness of these models, we should like to apply to them the evaluation of Lewis Carroll: "Whatever you say, the plan was splendid: it was simple and clear, you couldn't conceive of a better one. There was only one drawback to it: how it could be put into effect was totally unclear...."

At a reception for the participants at the 18th International Congress of Psychology in Moscow in 1966, the American scientist A. Rapoport stated that there are two forms of psychology.

"Firstly, scientific psychology, which utilizes all the methods of scientific research: experiments, modelling, etc. Secondly, so to speak 'interest psychology', which deals with deep psychological phenomena of certain people and organizations. For these phenomena, strictly scientific methods of research have not yet been worked out.... A question of the type: 'why did Ivan Karamazov so hate Smerdyakov: was it because the latter showed him his own ugly soul, or because Karamazov himself was like that...'
is impossible to solve by means of modern scientific psychology."
We fancy that the psychology of chess is first and foremost "interest psychology", and, probably, for this reason so much is still unknown in the entire sphere of forming and taking chess decisions.

The rich intellectual and emotional content of this sphere stems in particular from the combative nature of the game of chess. The point is that, in chess, it is not the white and black pieces which oppose each other, but player A, playing White, and player B, playing Black. Fictional terminology about "commanders, leading their armies and thrusting them into battle" are justified only when it is a question of the player, but not about the chess kings. Live chess, the game, is always "thinking for two", it is not a labyrinthine problem, where a selection or heuristic method can find a way out. Here "the strategy of play develops simultaneously in the minds of two different people" (Stefan Zweig), here it is necessary to adapt "your own plan to that of the opponent... and your ideas and fantasy are inevitably restricted, in the very nature of things, by the ideas and fantasy of another" (Alekhine). In chess "victory goes not to the one who plays well, but to the one who plays better" (Tartakover). All these observations are obvious, and for the moment are not subject to "scientific psychology".

In chess problems and studies, where the outcome is decided beforehand, as well as in positions of the type "find the best move", the active conflict situation is as though "degenerate", the conflict is arbitrary and no more resembles a genuine one than a conflict between different throws of a dice. A chess idea is put into reality by specifically chess means. (The specific nature of the chess "world" manifests itself if only in the obvious absence of a dependence between chess ability and creative ability in general; this was noticed by Zweig, but it is often forgotten by researchers into heuristics). But practical play always binds the thinking of a player and, moreover, forms it in a definite way. As Albert Einstein wrote in his introduction to the book on the life and career of Emanuel Lasker: "as a result of which the inner freedom of even the strongest person is inevitably destroyed." In a practical game there is a main point, determining the choice of decision, when a clash with the thoughts of the opponent occurs. He can impose his will on you, compel you to act in a certain way, and not otherwise, and can force you to look at the situation with his eyes. Or it can be just the opposite—there is a hope of subordinating the will and thoughts of the opponent. In making move "a", a player forces his opponent to reply with move "b" (since all other moves lose immediately), but move "b" allows move "c" to be made, to which the opponent is forced to reply with move "d", and so on. Each step brings him (the opponent!) closer to defeat, but he cannot avoid making this step. In this psychological interpretation, chess still awaits researchers.[1] When a player, on making his move, gets up and stands behind his opponent, he is attempting to look at the position through the latter's eyes, to penetrate into his thoughts. A player's assessment of the situation inevitably includes an assessment of the level of the opponent's pretensions (and of his own). What is he hoping for? And what do you yourself want—here, at this hour, in this game, in this tournament...?

It is from this position, and only this position, of "live chess", it seems to us, that one should look at the problems of decision and choice.

It would be a mistake to think that heuristic methods of chess playing are not known. Indeed, so as to master them, one requires ability, knowledge and experience. But a master has at his command an entire range of methods, he knows how to form a good plan, to see a good plan for his opponent, his brain is crammed full of recipes, gleaned from the well-written books of Capablanca, Vukovic and Lisitsyn. A master operates like a good chess program, until he is set an extra-difficult task—to win. He knows how to play, if he is happy to draw! But in

---

[1] Certain ideas on this problem will be developed by us in the following chapter.

chess it is not enough to play well, one must win. But books, after relating how to play simply and well, have not taught him how to seek the best, the very best, the one solution required for victory, the best idea, plan, variation, or move.

In any complex, dynamic situation it is unlikely that you will be faced with more than three possibilities. You can take positive action, or make a passive move, or choose a move which is neutral, passing on the problem, together with all the difficulties entailed, to the opponent. Although the choice of a neutral move may fully accord with a sensible evaluation of the mutual possibilities, it is justified only when there are genuine grounds for not making an active move. Otherwise a neutral move is a futile waste of time, for which both the spectator and the reader have to pay. In making a neutral move, you as though divest yourself of responsibility for any risk. And, perhaps, for you the price of such a move may prove to be extremely high in real terms (as in general in sport), but it should not be forgotten that we are toying with arbitrary values, and if there is no risk in the play, it is not worth a penny. Without risk there is neither victory, nor defeat. But a game which ends in a draw can turn into a defeat for both players.

That on which you base your choice is in any event associated with categories of risk and responsibility. These are concepts, which include moral components of activity, but not categories of heuristic searching. They lie in the field of "interest psychology".

There is one further aspect which explains the poverty of psychological content of interpretive, prognostic and other models. They do not include image phenomena, integral vision, and accompanying states of emotional intensity. Any block-diagram, any model, which divides a complete process into elements, impoverishes and distorts the real course of the process, in which the evaluation is always of an integral nature. Even the widespread concept of "correlation with a standard" is not exact. Of course, a chess master aims to correlate an "unknown", original position with a known one, for which there already are approved solutions. The set of such solutions retained in the memory is constantly replenished in the course of home preparation, the analysis of games, and so on. But correlation, comparison with a standard—this is again a discrete model, crude and superficial, since it does not embrace the processes of formation, transformation and recognition of images.

In the psychological analysis of a chess player's thinking we inevitably encounter two components which are normally opposed—vision and calculation, intuition and logic. Vision, remarked B. M. Blumenfeld, is "a passing of the end result through the centre of consciousness," a passing which is instantaneous. Calculation is a chain of operations, developing in time and recorded in external or internal speech, leading to a result. Integral comprehension, judgement, vision—these are intuitive acts, whereas calculation is the result of logical work. The contrast between intuition and logic runs like a thread through the study of creative thinking, including chess thinking. Poets and mathematicians, intuitive and logical brains, are to be found in chess history. Often a player who gravitates towards combinational solutions is automatically numbered among the calculating, logical brains; in contrast, the one who is inclined towards positional play is said to possess an intuitive cast of mentality. Sometimes these characteristics are wrong by 180°, if only when one is talking about Capablanca or Tal. It has to be said that it is hard to conceive of a less happy evaluation (but this is how many have written), to suppose that Tal possesses "electronic" capabilities of calculation, in contrast, supposedly, to intuition and fantasy. And it can confidently be stated that the contrasting of intuition and logic in chess is much less productive than in general in the analysis of creative activity.

Referring to image phenomena allows, as it seems to us, some sort of order to be introduced into the mechanisms of creative thinking, which are so conveniently and simply called intuitive. "Intuition is a rubbish tip onto which we pile all intellectual mechanisms, which we do not know how to analyze or even to name exactly, or of which the analysis and naming do not interest us," remarked M. Bunge. Although this author is in general inclined to make paradoxical assertions, in many instances one is inclined to agree with him. And nevertheless, by intuition the majority of people understand a quite definite process—a process of direct, rapid, instinctive if you like, comprehension or cognition, carried out without the help of logical deduction or reasoning. The same Bunge characterizes intuition as a normal method of thinking, based on the more developed abilities of rapid perception, imagination and evaluation. The rapidity of the intuitive process—this is its main distinguishing feature, thanks to which a new quality is acquired, and other psychological mechanisms appear. And it has to be assumed that, as was emphasized by B. M. Teplov, the rapidity of intuitive decisions is dependent upon previous preparation. Intuition discloses to the full extent the store not only of conscious, but also of subconscious experience. And this experience we extract in the form of images.

An image, as a mental representation of a source object, is a unique product of human consciousness. Computers operate without images. It is by means of images that decisions and actions are regulated, and that acquired experience is transformed into a creative idea (M. G. Yaroshevsky). Translated into the language of chess thinking, this idea was successfully expressed by St. Lem. Man is capable of

"an unusual dynamic integration: if he is a skilful player, then he perceives each individual piece arrangement as a definite continuous system, as something integral, possessing precisely expressed "branchable" tendencies of development.... A position which provides some formal emotional value is already regarded by the person as an *individualised whole*" [our italics—*the authors*].

The fact that the principles of decision making are different in a human and a computer has been pointed out by many. V. N. Pushkin, for example, wrote that in a computer the intuitive vision of a position is not reconstructed, and "the reflecting components of activity" are not put into reality. Man possesses, he emphasizes, the ability of "dynamic recognition", recognition through a transformation of the image of a situation. Very recently, similar ideas were suggested by Donald Michie, the well-known British specialist in artificial intelligence. His ideas, regarding image representation of information in a computer as the realization of the thinking mechanism of a chess player, will be touched on in chapter six. But here we emphasize: the essence of the matter is that the carriers of sense in chess thinking are "virtual" images of the real situation, transformed, existing only in the imagination, created by a process in which visual perception, memory and thinking are joined into one. "Losing the image means losing the sense," Paul Valéry remarked. These words can be fully applied to the object of our discussion.

The image is a necessary support for an idea. Creative thinking readily utilizes flexible and non-standardized systems of images, this is its inner supporting language, deeply individualized and hence creative. A genuinely talented player is distinguished first and foremost by his ability to operate by this language of images, accessible to him alone.

Visual images in solving processes play practically the leading role. Many oversights and blunders can be explained by the inertia of the visual image, its post-action, when, for example, a piece is still seen on a square, although several moves earlier it was exchanged. In a lengthy calculation in blindfold play, rapid dynamic images replace one another. Their depth, degree of structure and clarity are changeable and unsteady. Your thoughts are precisely directed—you are attacking f7, and thus you see an enormous, flickering black pawn and practically nothing else, the remainder of the board is obscured in mist. Your thoughts pick out and illuminate isolated parts of the board, groups of interacting pieces. Then they are once again released into the dark. Your optical system, visual memory, and visualization mechanisms operate at full power. It is the continuity of transforming visual images that provides the rapidity of intuitive thinking in particular, and the high quality of creative thinking as a whole.

Alekhine once described the principles of memory work in blindfold play.

"The player does not attempt to perceive before his eyes the entire board with its white and black squares, and white and black pieces . . . he recalls only some characteristic move, a configuration of a part of the board, similar to how in life we remember some acquaintance, book or thing."

This is an accurate observation. The chess player operates with aggregates of pieces and their configurations as individual psychological units. If you ask him, write Lindsey and Norman, to analyse a random, senseless arrangement of pieces on the board, "his wonderful memory and art of analysis disappear just as we lose the ability to remember a sequence of letters, if this sequence is lacking in meaning." It is the visually represented idea, the dynamic, transformable image, that is this integral psychological unit.

There are experimental confirmations of this. The Dutch scientist and chess player, de Groot, showed positions taken from real games to some examinees for a short time (5 seconds), then cleared the pieces from the board and asked them to restore the positions. Grandmasters and masters did this practically without error with 20–24 pieces on the board. Beginners were barely able to restore the positions of a few pieces. If the pieces were randomly positioned, the masters and the novices scored equally poor results. Similar experiments have been carried out by the Moscow physiologist V. Malkin. He said that, even when the presentation time was very short and the grandmaster (it was Alexander Tolush) was unable to restore the position, he could confidently decide: "White has the advantage" or "the position is level." This integral evaluation of the situation occurs before the differentiated perception and remembering of its elements. This is that intuitive grasping, that comprehension of the sense contained in the image of the situation formed by the person—as though over and above that image of perception given to him directly. This means that in the sphere of vision, visual perception and visual memory are included other, possibly logical, mechanisms, responsible for the "processing" of sense and its mental visualization. We emphasize this factor, because we do not see any other approach to the explanation of integrative properties of intuitive thinking.

In high-level chess thinking the image component, the complete structural vision of the properties of a chess position in movement, occupies a leading place. In this case, conceptual-vocal operations (for example, the recording of the process in terms of individual moves during calculation, in terms of notation), if they indeed have a place, are reduced or smoothed out. On the other hand, in the chess thinking of an amateur or a child the conceptual-vocal components are the main ones, and the pronouncing of moves and the discrete structure of decision taking are clearly expressed. "How do I know what I am thinking? I'll say, then I will find out," said the immortal Alice. This appeal to speech is confirmed by observations, and by self-made reports of play-ers. Moreover, when a master is tired, he resorts to a greater extent to "reasoning in chess notation". But in an active working state, when he is creatively stimulated, the master hardly resorts at all to this nota-tional (logical) method, in particular when searching for ideas and setting himself goals. He as though "gallops" past individual move opera-tions, and works with more large-scale semantic configurations, with integral units of thought. The master is for this reason a master, able to work at the level of integral units, in which he grasps the ideological and emotional value, determining the sense and weight of each individual move. As Antoine de Saint-Exupéry said:

> "A cathedral is by no means just a heap of stones. It is a geometric and architectural whole. It is not the stones which make up the cathedral, it is the cathedral's importance which gives value to the stones. . . ."

It should be mentioned that the dominant role of image-like, com-pletely structural integral components appears not only in the analysis of chess thinking. In modern mathematics one observes a tendency towards the creation of a new apparatus, which is less exact, meticulous, detailed and rigorous (E. S. Ventsel), a tendency towards operating with "diffuse" functions, especially for those problems associated with the computer modelling of human creative activity.

To the present day, many consider that the abilities of the chess player and the mathematician lie in the lengthy calculation of crystallized variations. But is this the case? To all appearances, these abilities are reflected rather in the ability to operate with "diffuse" functions. It would seem that a person is in general not capable of a "verbal" calculation at the board, and we do not find convincing attempts to attach consid-erable weight to calculating ability, which is then, supposedly, lost with age. Even grandmasters are not confident about the "quality" of calculation, since they are not able visually to comprehend a chain of variations. Judge for yourself the simple position in Figure 2. For a computer the calculation does not present any particular difficulty. But a person is not able to see and remember the 17–move manoeuvre by the queen. The moves by the queen to the right, to the left, up and

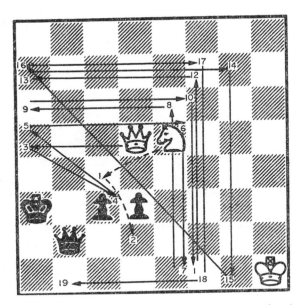

Fig. 2. Example of the solution to a position, in which for the erudite player there are no creative elements

White to move and win. Solution: **1 Nc4+ Ka2 (1 ... Kb3 2 Qb5+ Kc2 3 N×b2 d2 4 Nd1 K×d1 5 Qb1+ Ke2 6 Qc2 Ke1 7 Kg2 d1 = Q 8 Qf2 mate; 3 ... c×b2 4 Qc4+ Kd2 5 Qb3 Kc1 6 Qc3+) 2 Nd2+ (2 N×b2+ K×b2 3 Q×d3 c2—draw) 2 ... Ka1 3 Qa5+ Qa2 4 Q×c3+ Qb2 5 Qa5+ Qa2 6 Qe5+ Qb2 7 Qe1+ Ka2 8 Qe6+ Ka1 (8 ... Ka3 9 Nc4+) 9 Qa6+ Qa2 10 Qf6+ Qb2 11 Qf1+ Ka2 12 Qf7+ Ka1 13 Qa7+ Qa2 14 Qg7(d4)+ Qb2 15 Qg1+ Ka2 16 Qa7+ Qa3 17 Qf7+ Ka1 (17 ... Kb2 18 Nc4+) 18 Qf1+ Ka2 19 Qb1 mate.**

down are not associated with the designation of the moves, and are difficult to remember. Besides, Black's moves are monotonous, and the memory has nothing on which to grasp. But if the player knows or senses the possible final position, it merely remains for him to check the correctness of the intermediate branches (in the solution they are shown in brackets). Such situations rarely occur in practical games, where the main thing is to decide far in advance to go in for an initial position and to be able to drag the opponent into it. In one of Chéron's books on the endgame, there is a position where White has king, rook and bishop against Black's king and rook. White wins by elementary technical methods, but spends on this 156 (one hundred and fifty-six) moves! Who would undertake to calculate the variation in his head? (White: Kc6, Rf7, Bc4; Black: Ka8, Rh1. White to play.)

Corresponding to the rapidity of intuitive thinking and the creative potential concealed in it must be the rhythm, the tempo of play. It is in rapid play that the intuitive mind triumphs. Time provides an additional weapon for the player who is inclined towards slow, calculating play, and allows knowledge and factors of preparation to reveal themselves, rather than intuition, fantasy and daring. And yet practically all the top players possess a rapid, intuitive positional grasp. Why then does a game drag on for five tiring hours?

It is our deep conviction that a strong chess player requires only a few minutes of thought to get to the heart of the conflict. You see a solution immediately, and half an hour later merely convince yourself that your intuition has not deceived you. (Probably it is this that explains the mass attraction of lightning chess, or blitz. In blitz, all shallow, banal and uninteresting situations "gallop past" the mental glance. Even with a 5–hour playing session there are plenty of mistakes. And we are not at all in agreement with the assertion that blitz is "not chess", or that it is "another form of chess".) Why then do we force ourselves to think for scores of minutes at a time? It is evidently because, having time, an excess of time, we as though safeguard ourselves against erroneous decisions, and obtain a certain psychological confidence in the thought that we can eliminate any danger, and can foresee any threat. We do not think that a "predisposition" towards slow play has a different nature, or, as some suppose, that it depends on the type of "creative individuality", a "quick" or a "slow" mind.

But the psychological and creative losses from the many hours of "sitting" are immeasurably greater. Your intuition, on not receiving any "food", dies down, the flashes of fantasy fade, and the striving for risk irreversibly disappears. After all, it is not possible to retain in one's head a mass of sharp variations and solutions, dictated by artistic sense and conceived in the heat of inspiration. Your opponent experiences just the same. And as a result—tedious, unattractive, and also non-combative games, in which there is a clash not of rapid thought, talent and fantasy, but unwieldy pondering, burdened with a sense of avoidance of danger and of weighty preparation. But let us be fair. The best players in the world—Karpov, Larsen, Ljubojevic, Tal—are noted for their rapid play, perhaps instinctively sensing the importance of utilizing the very rich resources inherent in rapid intuitive thinking.

When a dialogue between a person and a computer is arranged, for some reason they study very carefully the specific nature of the problems solved by a person, so as to choose correctly the tempo of the dialogue, the time for the computer's reply. A delay in replying of more than 15 seconds is psychologically inconvenient for the operator. In chess, unfortunately, no one thinks about this.

The utilization of a high rhythm of play, its speeding up, is not only an instrument from the creative arsenal, so to speak. It is also a psychological instrument, a competitive weapon. In Zweig's *Chess Novelle*, it will be remembered, Mirko Chentovich sat immobile for a long time, staring at the board, so as to dislodge his opponent out of his lively, rapid rhythm of play, to force him to become nervous, to worry, and to lose interest in the game. It has to be said that Zweig conveyed very accurately this feeling of a loss of interest in the game by a person of bright, creative nature.

Time is required for the overcoming of a natural thinking inertia, for switching to another plan, another idea. But in 5 hours of play do we not create for this inertia such favourable conditions, that it fills up the entire process, essentially displacing the thinking itself? With slow play do we not lose the intrinsic fascination of chess, the ability to surprise with the unexpected, the ability to create? Remember the splendid lines of Vadim Shefner:

"Moment by moment, step by step,
You lapse into amazement,
All will be the same—and all not the same,
Within one instant."

Multi-hour games are monstrous, like dinosaurs from past ages. They kill lively thought, spread out in time the creative energy of the players (we will assume that these players still have "prejudices"). Twenty–three hours and 191 moves!—this was the length of the Pilnik-Czerniak game from the Mar del Plata tournament in 1950. It would appear to have gone down in history as a record for chess duration. In what other way could it have been remarkable? Insipid play in the opening, disorderly manoeuvres in the middlegame, and... a highly torpid endgame from the 60th to the 191st move, ending in a draw. After 60 moves this was the position: White: Ke1, Rd1, Bh5, pawns c3 and f4; Black: Kg7, Rb2, Be6, pawns c5, c4 and f5.

And here are some other monstrosities: Wolf–Duras, Carlsbad, 1907, 168 moves; Duras–Janowski, San Sebastian, 1911, 161 moves; Best–Bentsinger, Munich, 1934, 181 moves; Makagonov–Chekhover, Baku, 1945, 171 moves; and finally, if one is to believe the January 1972 issue of the Dutch chess magazine, in Tamper in 1971 a game was played between Ristoja and Neikopp, lasting 300 moves. The score of this super-giant was for some reason not published.... In our opinion, the adjournment of a game is in general contrary to the spirit of chess. It is pathology for creative competition. At one time they attempted to tackle this pathology. In the 1935 Moscow tournament, held in the Museum of Fine Arts, productive analysis was practically impossible, since the time allotted for the adjournment was 1 hour. Altogether there was 7 hours' play per day. In this tournament, Ragozin, attempting to combine supper with analysis, due to fatigue missed an easy win in his game with Capablanca.

The present-day organization of chess events does not, in our opinion, correspond to the psychological nature of chess creativity. It gives rise to negative feelings and to a certain extent is inhuman. You play one game. If you lose, you feel the urge to get even. You are in the power of noble emotions. But before you lie a long night and day, possibly two. Your thirst for battle dies away. And yet in this one, lost game you were unable to show your worth, demonstrate all that you are capable of, that you know. The obvious unjustness of the situation is oppressive. During this evening you could have played some four to six games with the same opponent, when misfortune and luck would have balanced each other. You would have had the energy to play interestingly, creatively, with enthusiasm.

For the readers who prefer to test arguments with facts, and also for those to whom it seems strange to have a chess book without chess, we will give the score of one particular game. It lasted... 1 minute, and was played in 1961 during an interval at a session of the USSR Chess Federation. Boris Spassky obligingly agreed to its publication.

White: *Bronstein*   Black: *Spassky*

1 d4 f5 2 e4 f×e4 3 Nc3 Nf6 4 f3 e×f3 5 N×f3 d6 6 Bf4 Bg4 7 Bc4 e6 8 0—0 Nc6 9 h3 B×f3 10 Q×f3 d5 11 Bb5 Bd6 12 Rael Kd7 (with a smile) **13 B×d6 c×d6 14 R×e6 K×e6 15 N×d5 N×d4 16 Qe3+ K×d5 17 Rf5+ Resigns (17 ... N×f5 18 c4 mate).**

A pure mate in the style of the Czech problem school! And all at 1–3 seconds a move....

This micro-flash of mutual fantasy afforded the grandmasters considerable joy, and the loser, Spassky, is happy to show the final position to his friends.

The question of playing rhythms deserves deeper consideration. The basis of it, of course, can only be formed by a time study of games by their time graphs. Following Blumenfeld, who as long ago as 1937 wrote of the importance of this work, we see the widespread, intelligent time study of games as an instrument of research work. Some 15 years ago, grandmaster David Bronstein suggested that the time spent on moves should systematically be recorded, and today we are happy to report that the time study of games is carried out in practically all major events. A vast amount of information has been accumulated, but essentially no-one has attempted to interpret it. One of the authors has devoted considerable time and effort to the analysis of chess time graphs. With certain preliminary results of observations regarding the development of games with time, we should like to acquaint the reader (in doing so, indeed, we are ready to bear all reproaches regarding the imprudence and hypothetical nature of our assertions).[2]

What can we learn from a time chart, this distinctive cardiogram of a chess game? Look at Figures 3–6. We will begin with the fact that, from the zig-zags in the lines it is immediately apparent whether the game was full of interest, or whether it was empty, like a piece of glass.

Fig. 3. Time graph of a "stitching-stitching" type of game (6th game of the Petrosian-Fischer match, Buenos Aires, 1971)

For two grandmasters with an inclination towards quiet play, the graph has the appearance of fine stitching—the deviations from the zero axis are very slight, and even where the rare impulses occur, it is difficult to see the slightest marked over-expenditure above the mean norm of 3–4 minutes. On the other hand, there are games whose cardiograms resemble lightning flashes in a severe thunderstorm. It has to be said that there is also a third variation, when there is a clash of players of the "impulse-stitching" class, when one sees lines of quick decisions and high bursts of mutual thought, a sharp conflict takes shape, the

[2] The games examined include many from Botvinnik's matches between 1954 and 1963, all the Candidates' Matches of 1965, 1968, 1971 and 1974, both Spassky–Petrosian matches, the Moscow International Tournaments of 1967 and 1971, the USSR Championships of 1967, 1969 and 1973, the 1973 Leningrad Interzonal Tournament, some 300 of Bronstein's games, and even a few games from the 1938 AVRO Tournament, for which a time study was made and published by B. H. Wood, editor of the English magazine *Chess*.

two sides readily enter into it, but promptly stop as if in perplexment as to what will happen next. Then the lines are repeated again, but now as though in a mirror reflection, then, as a rule, a new wave of high peaks ensues, and subsequent hollows already occur of their own accord, against the will of the players, since time trouble forces the play to be at a rapid tempo, corresponding now not to the maximum, but to the minimum. Of course, on a careful examination of such a graph, one can discover the nerve centres—the critical points of the game and the relative White and Black rhythms: each attempts to maintain his playing possibilities at the level of the opponent.

In principle, in each chess time graph one can see:

the line of opening play;

the reaction to an innovation;

an attempt to seize the initiative in the opening;

"instantaneous" lines in the opening, the middlegame and the endgame;

the commencement point of a player's own plan in the middlegame;

the starting point of a routine plan;

the starting point of playing for a win;

the reaction to a difficult move by the opponent;

the time spent on a set of moves;

a line of calculation for yourself, or for the two of you;

speed of thinking in the middlegame—in different types of position;

attitude to moves with a sacrifice—to your own and to the opponent's;

a search for active possibilities;

clearly visible peaks of attack;

smoothed over, but clearly defined lines of positional offensive;

dejected "stitching" in play where one is awaiting mistakes;

confident horizontal lines of good technique;

bow-shaped hollows in carrying out a long-range plan;

zig-zag lines of mutual combinations;

spasmodic beats of time trouble anxiety.

And, of course, much more besides.

5

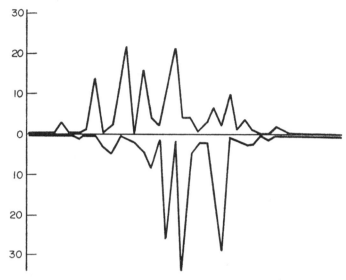

Fig. 4. Time graph of an "impulse-impulse" type of game (Reshevsky-Alekhine, AVRO Tournament, Holland, 1938)

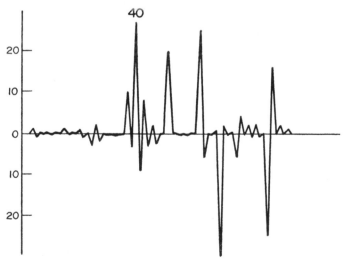

Fig. 5. Time graph of an "impulse-stitching" type of game (Smejkal–Karpov, Leningrad, 1973)

The authors suggest that non-chess players should skip the next few pages, and that players should examine on the board with us a typical encounter. The authors agreed that it would be better to explain something that is well familiar, and to this end have chosen the Bronstein–Larsen game from the Amsterdam tournament of 1964, a game between two players of similar creative style. Several annotations of this game have appeared in chess literature.

In the centre of the time graph (Fig. 7) is the zero line of instantaneous play, above it are the minutes spent by White on his moves, and below it the time in minutes spent by Black.

A general glance at the graph reveals two groups of high peaks, for White on moves 8–12, and for Black on moves 19–23. Does this mean that the difficult places for White were not difficult for Black, and vice versa? By no means. We have simply omitted to mention the subsidiary summits, 11–14 for Black and 18–24 for White. Black's peaks originate at the point where the White summits die down, while at the same time the secondary white summits have as though picked up from the main

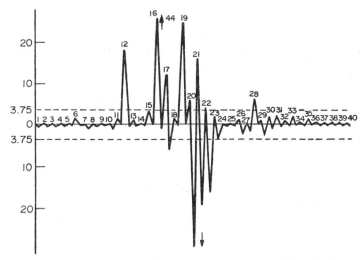

Fig. 6. Typical time graph of a sharp game, begun with a forcing variation. The figures along the axis indicate move numbers, and the dotted lines show the average interval of time allotted for each move (3.75 mins.)

5*

black peaks. In order to understand these regularities, it must be remembered that in a battle between two sharp players both want to win, but in the initial stage it is White who first rushes forward. This is why the peaks are often displaced.

In fact, there exists a diagonal symmetry, which becomes readily apparent if one examines a large number of graphs.

And so, White's first few moves were made with the intention of seizing the centre and obtaining a position with greater space. These are the confident lines 1–7. The burst at 8 is explained by an unexpected move, and the one at 9 by the possibility of several equivalent moves. The quickly-played move 10 was evidently the reason for the peaks 11–12, since on closer examination it turned out that the position, for which the players were impetuously heading, was complicated, and could obviously get out of hand. Therefore the slump at 13–17 indicates the collapse of White's opening plans. On the 16th move White enters into peace negotiations with the opponent, but without success; if anything, the initiative is already with Black. The peaks 18–19–20 are of an enforced nature. So as not to allow the opponent to develop his strategic offensive, White finds a latent combinational possibility for utilizing the strength of his rook on the seventh rank. Black's moderate bursts merely indicate that White's threats are not dangerous, since the

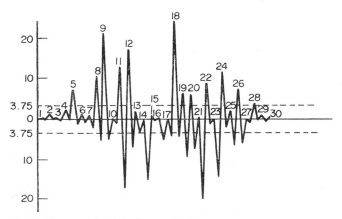

Fig. 7. Time graph of the Bronstein–Larsen game

maximum that the latter can achieve is to keep the position drawish. But when on the 21st move White faces his opponent with the necessity of choosing long concrete variations, Black spends the maximum amount of time in the present game on one move, since later it will be impossible to repair a mistake. Then the peaks gradually die down, which indicates that there are no longer any difficulties. However, it is just such a decay which often enables one to find a point where the opponent has not realized to the maximum the resources of the position. Since in parallel with the time graph we are giving an analysis of the chess situations, we notice fairly quickly that although line 25 seems to indicate resolution on White's part, the queen move itself is in fact weak. Meanwhile, lines 22 and 24 for White, and lines 21 and 23 for Black indicate rather that the position is full of energy, and that the solving of the combinations arising is by no means an elementary matter. Was White in time trouble? After all, often one plays quickly not because one wants to, but due to lack of time. No, he had 20 minutes, and in the resulting sharp situation White should have thought for at least 15 minutes. The position—which we give in the diagram of Figure 8—is the critical one of the entire game, and was precisely the one for which White was aiming, while Black too

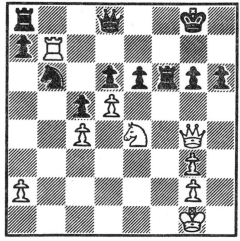

Fig. 8. The position in the Bronstein–Larsen game after Black's 24th move

did not object to it when he created his maximum time peak 21. So what in fact happened? An answer to this question is given by Larsen, so let us hear what he has to say:

"...on this natural move I spent 14 minutes, whereupon, like White, I had left barely half an hour. But while Bronstein was waiting for this move, he saw that he had overlooked something! He began to get nervous.... When I finally gave the check, Bronstein thought for 11 minutes; he had already practically lost his composure.... Panic stations! Out of his remaining 18 minutes Bronstein spent on this move only two, and in so doing abandoned his preliminary calculation. Of course, here two minutes is not an altogether correct estimate of the time spent, since the decision had already been taken while I was thinking.... Nerves, nerves, nerves. Unexpectedly Bronstein sees that which he had earlier overlooked, and this tense game is swiftly concluded...."

These extracts from Larsen's commentary are highly significant.

We are also bound to agree with Larsen regarding the fact that

"although Bronstein has written so much about this game, we still do not have a definitive explanation. Part of it reposes back in 1951, and another part in 1958.... In 1951 he was leading in a match for the World Championship with Botvinnik right up to the 23rd game. In 1958 he lost in the last round to the Filipino Cardosso, and failed to reach the Candidates' Tournament. Somewhere in his nervous system lie the scars from these defeats...."

(We should add that, now bearing the scar from Larsen, he lost in the 1973 Interzonal Tournament to a player who finished last, again lost at the decisive point of the tournament, and ended up behind the prize winners at a distance of that fatal one point, a point which migrates from tournament to tournament).

Let not the reader complain of the author's immodesty. Bear in mind that remembering a win is pleasant, but remembering a loss is vexing. Because in your neural "long-playing record" there are various grooves. And those places, where unpleasant information is stored, are better not touched. It is no accident that even the most outstanding players include in their game collections mainly brilliant wins, while their losses...

they leave behind among sets of tournament scoresheets. Willy-nilly, players have to study their lost games, so as to convince themselves... that they were winning. How much easier it is to remember them then! This is why Larsen annotated his win over Bronstein in the greatest detail of all the 50 games in his book, but could not refrain from... overestimating the critical position, and suggesting to the reader that White had to fight for a draw, although the variations—his variations— say the opposite.

White: *Bronstein*   Black: *Larsen*

1 d4 (0) **Nf6**(0) **2 c4**(1) **g6**(0) **3 Nc3**(1) **Bg7**(0) **4 e4**(2) **d6**(0) **5 Be2**(10)
0—0(1) **6 Bg5**(11) **c5**(2) **7 d5**(12) **e6**(4) **8 Nf3**(22) **h6**(8) **9 Bf4**(42) e ×d5(14)
10 e ×d5(43) **Re8**(15) **11 Nd2**(56) **Nh5**(32) **12 Bg3**(1.13) **Bg4**(39) **13**
0—0(1.15) N ×g3(41) **14 h** ×g3(1.15) B ×e2(57) **15 N** ×e2(1.17) B ×b2(57)
16 Rb1(1.17) **Bg7**(1.02) **17 R** ×b7(1.17) **Nd7**(1.06) **18 Nf4**(1.41) **Nb6**(1.10)
19 Re1(1.47) **Bc3**(1.19) **20 Ne4**(1.53) B ×e1(1.26) **21 Ne6**(1.53) B ×f2+
(1.46) **22 K** ×f2(2.01) f ×e6(1.47) **23 Qg4**(2.02) **Rf8**+(2.01) **24 Kg1**(2.12)
Rf6(2.03) **25 Qh3**(2.14) **Qf8**(2.08) **26 Ng5**(2.21) **Rf1**+ (2.14) **27 Kh2**(2.22)
Rf5(2.15) **28** N ×e6(2.26) **Rh5**(2.15) **29 Q** ×h5(2.27) g ×h5(2.15) **30**
N ×f8(2.27) R ×f8(2.15) White resigns.

Given in brackets is the time in minutes, and then in hours and minutes, spent by each of the players at the moment of giving the opponent the move—out of a total sum of 2 hours 30 minutes.

The authors are fervently in favour of chess time graphs, while fully recognizing the difficulties of their analysis. In the first instance it must be said that grandmasters never consider the position which they have in front of them. This means, that, except in the extremely stressful situation of time trouble, they do not think about the immediate move: they already know it. Grandmasters consider the consequences of this move within 1, 2, 3, 4, 5, etc., moves. They attempt—frequently they succeed in doing this, sometimes not—with a mental glance to follow the tracer lines of moves in the immediate variations, and, after sifting the resulting positions through a sieve of instant evaluation, attempt to

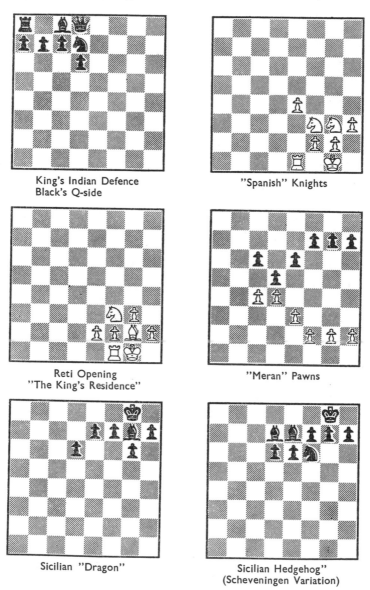

King's Indian Defence
Black's Q-side

"Spanish" Knights

Reti Opening
"The King's Residence"

"Meran" Pawns

Sicilian "Dragon"

Sicilian Hedgehog"
(Scheveningen Variation)

Fig. 9. Any one of these patterns provokes in a player memories of hundreds of games played with these openings

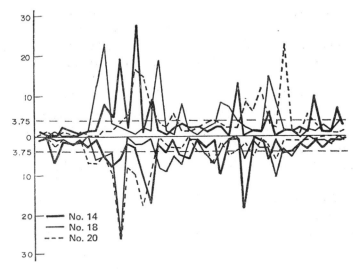

Fig. 10. Time graphs of three games from the 1957 Smyslov–Botvinnik World Championship Match, played with the French Defence

perceive where, in which direction, it will be easier to carry out this or that offensive idea, organize a stubborn defence, or set the opponent a more difficult creative or technical problem. It is here that the most important side of chess talent lies—in the ability to see without the board.

We should like to draw attention to the fact that memory enables us quickly to make moves in situations, which, taken on their own, require lengthy thought, since they do not have a single solution, but in practice have already been solved and tested by others. This applies not only to the opening, but also to the middle stage of the game, which also has the characteristic of repeating itself for different players with only small deviations, which do not influence the overall pattern of the position. What is this pattern of a position? We can give the following answer—it is the main group of pieces and pawns, comprising a striking force, the key element in organizing attack or defence. In such cases, insignificant changes in the arrangement of the secondary forces do not have any essential influence on the plan of play and the general evaluation of the position. Such a pattern is often simply a routine thing, and players know many routine patterns in various openings. It is sufficient to show only the outlines of the white or black pieces alone, and one can guess from which opening the position is taken (Fig. 9). The reason is that each opening has its own standard contours, its own routine patterns, and here we see that play proceeds with the help of sets of moves, the lengths of which are different for different openings. From the graphs it is evident that players do not think about their immediate moves, but about the pattern of the position as a whole, and about their projected plans. The plans, of course, have to be corrected at each move: hence the confident straight lines and unexpected leaps of dense vertical lines—corrections are being made.

To conclude our protracted discussion of time graphs, we must point out that the graphs themselves also have their stable contours, characteristic of different openings. For example, in the Ruy Lopez there are at first two long lines for White and for Black, then at approximately the 15th move one of the lines makes a swift leap upwards, provoking a similar reaction on the part of the opponent. Alas, within a few moves

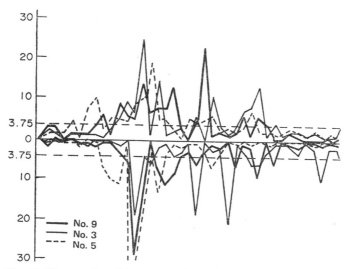

Fig. 11. Time graphs of three games from the same match, played with the King's Indian Defence

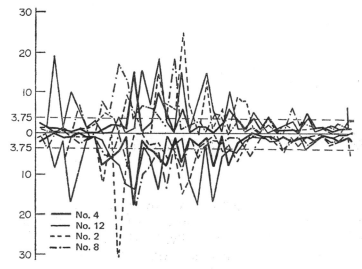

Fig. 12. Time graphs of games from the same match, played with the Sicilian Defence

the bursts die down, and either peace is concluded, or else someone will have lost. In the Sicilian Defence, on the other hand, we see sharp peaks for White and for Black, lasting for five to seven moves, and this nerve centre eats up almost all the time allotted for the 40 moves. It is the same in the French Defence, but there the onset of the nerve centre comes later and is not so clearly defined. In the Caro–Kann Defence everything goes smoothly up to the middle, then there is a burst of one or two moves, and again quiet. On the fifth or sixth move the Himalayas of the King's Indian lines arise, whereas the Queen's Gambit is accompanied by rare impulses. Take a look at our graphs (Figs. 10–12), where for some things you will have to take our word. All the same, the persuasion of people is based to a large extent on frequent repetition....

CHAPTER 5.

Individual against Individual

IN CHESS, as in any other field of creative activity, the manifestation of individuality is as necessary as it is natural. And at the same time there is in chess the danger of losing originality, individuality. Nevertheless, every great chess player is an individual, with a distinctive peculiarity of mentality and character. Intensity of thought in chess is intensity of the entire spiritual, inner aspect of a person. In this aspect everything is fused: the richness of imagination, impetuosity of decision and action, attitude to spiritual and moral values, individuality of character, and social dynamism of the individual. In this aspect tragic notes are sometimes heard (Einstein on Lasker), at times it is complex, incomprehensible and improbable (Fischer), sometimes it is concealed behind an impenetrable mask of simple-mindedness (Karpov), or of demonism (Tal). But always and everywhere in chess there is a clash of individuals, and the aim and sense of their behaviour are determined by the inexorable laws of the struggle.

Emanuel Lasker wrote:

"Every kind of battle is only apparently different. The laws governing them are always identical. In this sense war is regarded as a competition, a pursuit of truth, beauty or happiness; all these forms of battle are similar one to another, and also to the game of chess."

In our day this openly combative content has been strongly confirmed in everything relating to psychological aspects of chess. Whether it is a question of a tense elimination event, of the preparation for a tournament or for a meeting with a specific opponent, of the planning or analysis of action—here, there and everywhere we encounter the psychological factors of the struggle, and it is they that paint in a single tone the inner aspect of an individual, unique, like a fingerprint.

Journalism eagerly imitates the vocabulary of conflict, battle, encounter, etc. Respected publications write: "a cold-blooded assassin at the chess board" (about Larsen), "a vampire with a fixed, burning glance" (about Fischer), and so on and so forth. All this is lyricism, and good luck to the journalists. But when after a game (take any elimination match) the players, after shaking hands, depart without analysing the concluded game, so as to avoid disclosing by chance some secret of preparation, this is something worth thinking about.

Perhaps the most significant feature of the present-day "sharpening of the struggle" in chess is the adoption of scientific-psychological methods of preparation. It will be no exaggeration to estimate that the outcome of a game depends only 25 per cent on its actual course, while 75 per cent of it is determined by lengthy and well-organized preparation. What is needed for such preparation? Grandmaster Averbakh and psychologist Kossov reply:

"First and foremost self-control, the control of your state of mind. For this keep a diary, assess your condition, carry out objective measurements, test yourself. Ask yourself questions before the start of a game and after it, measure your pulse rate, count your hours of sleep, and so on."

These authors are confident that the accumulation of data on objective control, self-assessment and game results will enable you "to disclose the causes of the result achieved in a game, and outline a path of possible correction of the training process." Ah, if only the secret of victory or defeat lay in "the accumulation of data"! And even so, one should not underestimate certain, possibly naïve and simple recommendations, which professional psychologists can suggest.

More important and more interesting is the following. Mikhail Levidov, to whose ideas we have already frequently referred, openly declared that "since there is a complete lack of investigation into either the individual biographies, or especially the social biographies of the majority of great chess players, one is obliged to grope in the dark and, to a considerable extent, to introduce elements of surmise and conjecture into attempts at analysis." Even today, as we see it, attempts to reflect biographical elements in the creative portrait of a chess player remain at the level of conjecture. Possibly the one exception is the book by Viktor Vasiliev. Zweig's World Champion Chentovich has no prototype in life, and remains merely a literary hero "for contrast". But of undoubtedly genuine interest would be the analysis of a real, complex situation, with a chess clash between people of different ages, different social and individual life experience, with different emotional traits, and different ambition and faith in themselves. The struggle brings together fighters, hardened in many years of battles and with scar-covered nervous systems, against young people, as yet poorly protected from life, and only just commencing their careers in big-time chess; or people with an assured position and intellectual laziness against dissatisfied, ambitious people, who see in chess the one way of achieving success in life. Each has his worldly wisdom. Does not chess creativity reflect it? We realize that we are asking too many questions. This will get us nowhere.

We do not know the answers, and are convinced that to answer them is more difficult than to measure a pulse or even to force the player himself to answer.

While speaking of the more than modest achievements of chess psychology, we cannot help recalling the first researches by Diakov, Petrovsky and Rudik, carried out during the Moscow International Chess Tournament in 1925.

Essentially, the psychologists were seeking an answer to one question: what physical and mental qualities are required of people, striving to achieve success in chess? Diakov compiled a psychogram (professiogram) of a player, in which he included 16 superior qualities. And while 50 years ago things were said about thinking and imagination that from today's point of view seem naïve or controversial, indisputable is the high evaluation of properties that are "professionally important for a chess maestro, and, therefore, for anyone interested in the game of chess," such as a good reserve of physical strength, strong nerves, self-control, the ability to direct one's attention, a disciplined will, discipline of emotions, belief in oneself. . . .

For outstanding results today, even more necessary for a player than talent are "character, special preparation and a robust nervous system, capable of hard work" (Botvinnik). "A person must have the character of a fighter to become a good chess player."—Larsen echoes him. Amazing coolness and self-control—these are the exceptional traits of fighting character which reward (and rightly so) Lasker and Karpov. "Chess is not for the faint-hearted."—these famous words of Steinitz reflect best of all the character of the struggle in chess. A strong character, resolution and constant readiness for an uncompromising struggle— these are rare gifts, although no more rare than talent, especially in our competitive age, and life in an atmosphere of world-wide competition. The character of a fighter is, of course, not a unique concept. It was easy for Theophrastus, in the 4th century B.C., to designate character (it was from him, incidentally, that this term originated) by a single feature—"pretence" "flattery", and so on. The character of a fighter is, of course, a blend of outstanding qualities, but isn't there something unwordly about the fact that we take to task a young pioneer, who has burst out crying after losing a game in a team event, for the reason that he is not a fighter (a fact from a report of the "White Rook" competition, published in the newspaper *64*)? And why do we say nothing about the character of a creator?

However, it is not worth accusing our time of competitive-psychological maximalism. Perhaps it was chess which paved the way for it into big-time sport in general. Back in 1927 Alekhine expressed in exact terms the doctrine of "individual against individual". He wrote:

"There is something in which our generation of chess players—who have reached roughly the age of forty—is superior to the old masters (with the exception of Lasker): not only cunning, which is often merely a sign of weakness of character, but also the conviction acquired with experience that for chess, for the chess struggle, is necessary first and foremost a knowledge of human nature, an understanding of the psychology of the opponent. Formerly the struggle was only with the pieces, whereas we struggle (or at any rate attempt to

struggle) with the opponent—with the enemy, with his will, nerves, with his individual peculiarities, and—last but not least—with his vanity."
A fine, if somewhat abstract thought. In our day it has taken on a concrete form, which applies also to actions of international competitive renown.

In the opinion of Tal (his observations are not only interesting, but also correct), Fischer's behaviour in the 1972 match was devised and planned by a highly qualified psychologist, although it was risky to a high degree.[1] After Fischer's failure to appear for the second game, Spassky had to "sit and think, what in fact was the score in the match." It was this episode from the second game which probably made standard, so to speak, the atmosphere of psychological pressure, aimed at strictly individual features of the character of Spassky, for whom it is difficult playing against an opponent who is disagreeable to him (an observation by A. Samoilov). This is a conscious way of disturbing the opponent's mental balance, and stronger than those which are to be found in the old books of Damian or Lopez: "Let the sun shine in your opponent's eyes.", "if you are playing by candle-light, let the candle burn to the right hand side of your opponent", and so on. Nowadays, all conceivable factors of personality are laid on the scales. In addition, present-day fighters have numerous non-chess methods of damaging the nervous system. Too dynamic is the environment, which intensively and not always regularly affects the character, mood and mental state of a person.

And besides, the very course of a game is full of inner nervous tension. Just try overcoming the will of the person sitting opposite you for five long hours, without once looking him in the eye, except at the moment of shaking hands—such are the demands of ethics. The battle plan has been composed and re-drawn a hundred times, and now in the opening, quickly and carelessly moving the pieces, inwardly the grand-

[1] In the opinion of the American grandmaster Reuben Fine, at the heart of Fischer's behaviour before, during and after the match with Spassky lay "emotional conflicts with himself and with the chess world." Fine's ideas are, of course, not especially original, and are merely a crude projection of Freudian schemes onto the behaviour of the participants in the match.

master is concentrating extremely hard, so as to avoid making a different move, one which is even excellent, but which has not been planned beforehand. Ten, fifteen moves—neither side has used more than a minute, but now the situation becomes more and more tense: one of the two is winning the battle—within a move or two is reached a position which in preparations for the game has been thoroughly studied and played out to the bare kings. It is here that the nerves give way.... And it is not often that the proud, courageous words of Lasker, uttered by him before his match with Rubinstein in 1913, are justified:

"During the course of the match, I expect that several times victory will smile joyfully on each of us, and several times defeat with its cold, evil eyes will stare us in the face, but neither of us, one must expect, will on account of this lose his self-control."

Unfortunately, or perhaps fortunately, individual traits of personality have as yet only slightly been subjected to analytical dissection. We have many oddities which go to make up our outward, and also our inner appearance. You may be irritated by your opponent's gaudy tie, and if he should hold his teacup in both hands, this is simply unbearable. You become irritated by having to queue at the buffet, and also, if you will pardon us, the toilet. The most insignificant trifle, which tomorrow you will have forgotten forever, today worries you, forces you to walk a little more quickly than usual across the stage, but this is today, when the most efficient, the most exact work is required of you. We are all living people, sensitive and impressionable. Some heatedly and loudly share their emotions with those around, others keep silent. A mask of indifference and of detachment from everything wordly is on the face of Karpov. But Viktor Vasiliev is right: the indifference is also a mask. In our little and not so little habits are the traces of years lived, of feelings experienced. It is good that psychologists have still to discover these traces. And, incidentally, to reveal in passing, is it true or not that Tal hypnotizes his opponents...?

It is in peoples' make-up that they forget their joys much more quickly than their sorrows. In 1966, Petrosian, commenting on his first and successful match with Spassky, remarked that, in contrast to certain players, after a failure he never tormented himself with reproaches.

6

Petrosian is most probably an exception to the rule. It is hardly possible to conceive of a more obsessive thought, than the thought of defeat, of an oversight, of a missed opportunity. You failed to play 29 Ra7!, and you remember this for a long, long time, just as you remember how once you failed to kiss a girl, and that, who knows, changed your whole life. You try to persuade yourself: enough, it is all in the past, but within ten minutes you again sink into a mire of bitter memories, and aimlessly torment yourself.

How good it would be if our experiences merely accompanied us like an incorporeal shadow. But that's not the way it is. It is our emotional life which regulates the game of chance. "Fortune favours the strong" runs the Latin proverb. As Spielmann once remarked, what we must understand by this is strength of character. But strength of character and strength of feeling are different things. For chess players, to some extent, these strengths are inversely proportional. No-one can yet explain the bad blunders and oversights by great masters, committed not under the stress of time trouble, but for no apparent reason, and after due consideration. Then they say: "he had a mental black-out," and there is perhaps no other way of classifying this failure of the thinking apparatus. Spielmann used to call it 'bad luck'. For such fantastic blunders the Germans have a rather appropriate term: "Fingerfeller"— a mistake of the fingers, or in its Latin version, "lapsus manus". The "specialist" in such mistakes can probably be considered the Hungarian grandmaster Szabó, who many times in his long tournament career has picked up the wrong piece. And here it is a matter not of absent-mindedness, and not of loss of concentration. Do you remember—in Yevgeny Oniegin?

> "They meet, from others far retreating,
> Above a game of chess they bow,
> Now heads on elbows resting, now
> In deepest mediation sitting,
> A pawn of Lenski's takes a rook,
> His own, if he did care to look."[2]

[2] The translator is indebted to Mr Henry Jones, of Riding Mill, Northumberland, for this translation from Pushkin's novel in verse.

It is more of a question of emotional state, of the constant emotional background, which can unexpectedly break out into an incomprehensible, rationally inexplicable "mistake of the fingers". Attempts to classify bad blunders, by finding for them a different, chess cause ("the forgotten piece", "the disappearing square", etc.), as was done long ago by Ilyin-Zhenevsky and in our time is being done by Krogius, are undoubtedly interesting, but the psychological nature of mistakes here remains completely unexplained. Of course, references to the emotional sphere are not very instructive, but they do at least indicate the direction in which to look. And our barely perceptible mistrust of the efforts of psychologists studying chess has as its source the iron logic of Spinoza: "The only reason people consider themselves free is that they are conscious of their actions, but the causes which determine these actions they do not know."

It should be mentioned that many researchers abroad (Fine, Schönberg and others), to explain the psychological aspects of chess, resort to crude speculations, reducing essentially to a repetition of the ideas of Adler and Freud, which used to be fashionable early in the present century. "Chess is an outlet for the aggression of man", "the attractiveness of chess is explained by its symbolic projections into the sexual sphere", and so on. The authors of these assertions openly exploit the present mass interest in chess and in the study of individual personality. The clash of personalities in chess is of course a complex phenomenon, and to explain this complexity "outside" chess itself is evidently not possible. Attempts to formulate explanations beyond the bounds of the chess board would be of scientific value, provided that they did not reduce to excessively narrow and unproductive schemes of psychoanalysis, as in the works of Fine and others.

Virtually the most modern and the most complete expression of the clash of personalities in chess is the attempt to imitate an idea or decision of the opponent, and force him to act in a definite way, favourable, of course, to yourself. Such a directing of the opponent is sometimes called reflex.[3] The frequently-occurring bluff is merely one of the forms of reflex directing.

In reflex directing the opponent is given certain information, the idea of which is usually as follows: to influence the mental and emotional states of the opponent, and to affect his capacity for work. Information can be transferred at the level of indistinctly realizable influences, at the level of "sensing". "It must be instilled in the opponent that he is weaker," says Karpov. The degree of confidence of your play, and your rapidity and resolution make the opponent become nervous. He thinks (or "senses") that you know how you should play. And you think, that he thinks, that you know how you should play, and you assume an expression of indisputable confidence in victory. Sometimes you act in the opposite way, and with your dejected appearance demonstrate that you are doomed, or that you are happy with a draw. Botvinnik, and after him Viktor Vasiliev (cf. *Teatr, 1974,* 8), has told quite openly of acting ploys of this type. On arriving for the adjournment of one of his games, Botvinnik controlled his outward behaviour in a definite way (on this occasion even his celebrated thermos flask was left behind), so as to suggest to Tal that the outcome of the game was decided, and that the adjournment would conclude quickly. This trick, aimed at weakening the vigilance and capacity for work of the opponent, is often encountered. There was a forerunner to Botvinnik. In the last round of the 3rd Moscow International Tournament in 1936, Capablanca, a well-known lover of ballet, placed on the table his tickets for the theatre. His entire appearance proclaimed that he desired nothing more than to conclude the game as quickly as possible and to set off to the theatre. His opponent, grandmaster Eliskases, expecting a draw, weakened very slightly, and... Capablanca brilliantly won a very difficult ending. However, nowadays such tricks happen more and more rarely. Chess players have sized up one another, and know well their individual traits of behaviour and their unexpected deviations.

---

[3] One of the authors of this book used the term "reflex directing" back in 1968, cf. for example, "Algebra Konflikta" ("The Algebra of Conflict"), *Znanie,* Moscow, 1968.

The transfer of information in reflex directing can also pursue other aims, in particular, a direct influence on the forming of an idea and plan by the opponent, on his choice of decision, and in the end on the directing of the struggle into a channel which is logically and psychologically uncomfortable for the opponent. Here it is all as in war. In chess too, the player who is being attacked is inclined to overestimate his opponent's threats (the threat is always stronger than the execution). Frightening and "pressurizing" of the opponent are also carried out openly (demonstration of intentions, etc.). Masking, sharp changes in plan, neutralization of the opponent's plan, exploiting lack of time—all these devices have been borrowed by chess players from the sphere of the "armed struggle". Play is often concentrated around positions of unstable equilibrium, which suit both sides up to a certain time. This unstable equilibrium can be resolved by an explosion or by a tacit mutual agreement between the two sides. The choice of decision in such positions is especially difficult and committing, and therefore a player often tries to lure his opponent into just such a position. A player, who in practical play is able to form and carry out dozens of reflex directing ploys, considerably raises his chances of winning. Authors of new chess text books, if they wish to be abreast of the times, should not avoid also including these ploys. Or perhaps it would be sufficient to analyse, but from a new point of view, the splendid old books by Lasker, Capablanca, Nimzowitsch and Euwe.

The authors beg the reader to take note of the reflex interpretation of chess struggle psychology. Matches for the World Championship are played not by novices, but by professional specialists in the very highest meaning of these words. For grandmasters the chief difficulty is not to guess the type of position, or to discover a combinational blow or a means of constructing a wall of pawns. The modern grandmaster is laden with practical, technological devices, like a banana-tree with bananas. The question is rather different. What to use out of the abundance of these devices, what to employ earlier and what later, how will the opponent react to this or that device. And by no means the last place in these thoughts (and feelings) is occupied by reflex reasoning.

Reflex directing devices, based on a purely chess content, are of course a natural weapon of struggle, like other technical methods. But devices of a behavioural content, influencing the mental sphere, based on deceipt and falsehood are, in our opinion, immoral and dangerous. This must be said openly, without making any accusations. It is the more important for the reason that even people who are competent at chess do not distinguish altogether distinctly chess and non-chess ploys of struggle. Thus Petrosian considers that "an incorrect sacrifice [that's all!—*the authors*] and other ploys of a similar nature, which mislead the opponent and promise unlawful success", are a manifestation of pragmatism. It is difficult to suspect the Ex-World Champion of being naïve, more likely this is simply an unwillingness to speak openly of means of achieving an "unlawful success" in a competitive struggle. After all, an incorrect piece sacrifice is one thing, but it is quite another to play with an outward appearance and imitation, reflecting "mental shock".

The question of the social and ethical evaluation of falsehood in competitive events is a complex one, and any plebiscite would show a spectrum of different opinions—from categorical rejection to categorical approval. We are on the side of the former. Immoral falsehood is no less obvious than immoral prompting. What is surprising is that to deny a charge of prompting is considered a matter of honour (chess history is full of such examples), whereas deception, or to put it mildly, misleading by means of deceptive play, can be written about almost with affection.

It should not be forgotten how great is the moral lesson of an honest struggle. Cultivating in children a love for the splendid and a respect for the partner (not the opponent!), staunchness of spirit and an ability to endure misfortune, self-criticism and spiritual generosity, we must concentrate our attention on precisely these psychological qualities, the qualities of a worthy person. Chess should not become something of a vital examination, which one must pass at all costs. Play to your heart's content, for your enjoyment, and for that of your teachers and parents, and be honest and noble in this game and in this struggle.

CHAPTER 6.

On the Way to the Electronic Grandmaster

GRANDMASTERS and masters examine with condescending interest games played by programs. "In our time our chess will suffice," they remark, "However, this is not our business". Specialists in artificial intelligence, on the modelling of problem-solving processes on the computer, see in chess programs a fruitful field of research, although on the whole they are not inclined to overrate either the successes achieved, or the apparent prospects. Journalists and science and chess commentators respond hurriedly to competitions between programs, and professionally excite the general public with assessments and forecasts, which for the most part contradict one another. And public opinion is formed little by little out of all these conflicting assessments, although it is true that there is nevertheless an overriding mood of optimism—such is the atmosphere of scientific fetishism in which we all live.

Recently *Literaturnaya Gazyeta* (*4,* 1975) decided, in full accordance with the canons of modern journalism, to put a traditional question to the six living Ex-World Champions: "Will an electronic grandmaster be created?". The opinions of the former Champions were divided—as is supposed to happen according to these canons. Adamant optimism and the authority of a Doctor of Technical Sciences were to be heard in the opinion of Mikhail Botvinnik— it will! The other specialist (in his youth a professional mathematician), Max Euwe, admitted that computers were playing more and more strongly, and even expressed regret at this, but avoided giving a direct reply. Our remaining grand-masters, educated in the humanities, of course, gave vague replies, and only Boris Spassky, who honestly admitted that he was not competent to answer, immediately avoided any discussion. Vasily Smyslov an-swered in the negative, alluding to the fact that only man possesses original thinking. Tigran Petrosian expressed his scepticism, but, ev-idently recalling the first World Championship for chess programs in the summer of 1974, added that he did not rule out competitions between computers, and of course, competitions between people. And Mikhail Tal simply hopes that there will be no electronic grandmaster, since otherwise the number of chess followers will be reduced, since no one will be interested in absolutely faultless play. Thus, with the help of the Ex-World Champions, *Literaturnaya Gazyeta* once more drew our attention to one of the burning questions of present-day scientific and technological development. Perhaps it is merely from simple vanity that we are convinced that we play (and will play) better than a computer? Or perhaps Stanislav Ezhi-Lets is right, in promising that "technology will soon achieve such perfection, that man will be able to manage without himself"?

Once upon a time, a man concealed in a box played chess against Napoleon. In those distant times no one had any suspicion of the pow-erful forces of the mechanized twentieth century. Many strong chess players took part in the hoax with the box, and, not without reason, out of approximately three hundred games played they lost only six (Napoleon was defeated by Allgaier, one of the strongest Viennese masters; remember the Allgaier Gambit?). Today the successes of the computer appear mystical. They, indeed, do not exactly fit into the natural order of things for mere mortals (Norman Weiner). But the electronic filling of present-day boxes is a reality. And today we feel that, to all questions of the type "can the computer do this?", a positive answer should be given.

Probably one of the most fascinating aspects of modern computer chess is the possibility of competition between man and machine. The steel robot with doors in its belly and inflexible knees is not, of course, a rival to man, except when it is necessary to lift heavy loads or to rush along a fantastically burning-hot wasteland. Human and electronic brains—that is another matter. Even to some broken electrical connection in a computer one can seek an analogy in the human nervous system, where, however, connections are broken much more frequently. Let us discard, for the moment, arguments that the computer is the product of man's mind and skill, as well as all considerations of a humouristic vein. Let us place our rivals in equal conditions. Surely this is a remarkable event in the history of man: the intellect of man can be cleansed of its human casing, weighed up, measured, and evaluated by usual human standards. It is in such a competition that we can clearly appreciate how far we have progressed in our understanding of intellect and the human mind, and appreciate how little we yet know about thinking, about man, and... about playing chess. Of course, we do not identify ourselves with the computer, except perhaps as regards "the degree of ignorance of processes taking place" (G. Tsopf). But from our human nature we are inclined to believe obvious results, rather than obscure premises. This is why we are so excited, when we hear of a computer playing chess, irrespective of whether it is playing a human or a similar machine.

Many consider that chess is an ideal medium for the study of artificial intelligence. Everything that human reason is rightly proud of, and in particular, the ability to foresee the consequences of decisions taken and to plan its actions, is utilized in programming. But it is not clear whether or not a program which plays chess can rightly be called intelligent. It is comparatively, selectively intelligent—in the sense that it is totally unsuitable for the solving of other intellectual problems, for example the solving of differential equations, just as any program for the solving of differential equations is useless for playing chess. But human intelligence, as Donald Michie rightly remarks, is characterized by its versatility and by the ability it displays in the most diverse fields. In general the question of the intelligence of a chess program in direct form is an academic one, and there is no straightforward reply to it. Whether we set ourselves logical criteria (ability towards classification, generalization, recognition of images, induction, etc.) or whether we will judge on the output of the "black box"—the final result of play, whether we will scrupulously seek creative components in its decisions or will be satisfied with its ability to learn—we are unlikely to reach a convincing reply, since, after all, we as yet know so little about our own, human intelligence, and in any event we have no other non-human criteria of intelligence, although, as life suggests, we have human criteria in excess.

Even more complicated is the question as to whether a chess program can ever play creatively, with fantasy, with imagination, with a "spark of God", and similar human qualities. Academician A. N. Kolmogorov once said quite definitely: so as to teach a computer to write good verse, one must program into it the entire history of human civilization. The content of our concepts is determined by our attitude to them, said another top mathematician, A. A. Markov, therefore our assessments of both machine and human creativity are always associative and emotional.

And at the same time they are not at all as exact as they would like to be. What can one do: the question of the creative character of a program's play is simply pushed into the background. We study heuristic thinking mechanisms, we will systemize the experience, we will test various principles of program compilation, said John McCarthy, head of the work on game programming at Stanford University, during the first Soviet–American match between chess programs in 1967–68. But already then they ceased in principle to identify the concepts—heuristic and creative. Nowadays the approach is notable for being even more efficient, a player is now compared with an economic manager (V. A. Trapeznikov), and the concept of a complex creative problem simply characterizes a level not yet achieved by programmers.

Nevertheless we are all confident that the programming of the game of chess is directly related to the problem of artificial intelligence. We value the possibility of evaluating objectively the tempo of our progress towards the solving of this "problem of the late twentieth century", comparing the strength of programs with human intellect according to flexible and differentiated criteria. Finally, we find highly appealing the intensive environment of searching, mystery and audacity in which chess programmers work. We are all, without exception, both dreamers and realists.

"They say to us "madman and dreamer",
But escaping from melancholy dependence,
In time the skilful brain of a thinker
Will create an artificial thinker."

Goethe: *Faust*

In August 1974, it will be remembered, the Soviet chess program *Kaissa* was victorious in four games, and our scientists were awarded a 110-gm gold medal by the International Federation of Information Processing, with the inscription "World Computer Chess Championship". This fairly recent experiment showed that all programs are at any event based on the principle of variation analysis. The difference in the strengths of the programs is explained by the completeness, and, if one can express it so, the degree of correspondence between the principles laid down in this analysis, and the character of the positions which actually occur in a game. This latter factor signifies that a program can play certain positions very strongly, whereas in others it begins to "flounder". For a number of positions the actual depth of calculation (for example, 5 half-moves ahead, as *Kaissa* used to play) may not be sufficient, while auxiliary devices—say, for calculation in forcing variations—may simply not be used in a case where the weight of positional factors is very great. There is therefore a certain element of "competitive luck" in the play of chess programs. A program may hit upon those positions, those ideas, for which it is well prepared, and use its opening library to the fullest extent. But it also may not. In a certain sense, *Kaissa* was fortunate. In the deciding game with the American program *Ostrich* it made an elementary blunder and lost the exchange: to economize on time, it had been restricted to a calculation of only three half-moves. *Ostrich*, in turn, was unable to win by a combination with a rook sacrifice, for the calculation of which nine half-moves were required. In general, this "World Championship" confirmed once again the practical inexhaustibility of chess positions, and to some extent the fundamental limitations of the methods used in programming.

The history of chess programs begins with the work of Claude Shannon, published back in 1950. Shannon did not propose a program, but he examined the basic problems arising here. According to Shannon, chess is a game with a finite number of possible positions, and for each position there is a finite number of possible moves. The rules of the game guarantee that within a finite number of moves either a win, a loss or a draw will be achieved. One can therefore give a description of the play by means of a "tree", the tops of which correspond to the positions and the branches to the possible moves. It is intuitively obvious that, for a player who can survey the entire tree as a whole, and see the most distant consequences of each decision taken, chess will become an easy game. Shannon suggested that in the analysis of the tree of play one should be guided by the following principles: firstly, examine all possible moves to a fixed depth; secondly, give a numerical evaluation to the moves; thirdly, use for this evaluation weighting points, ascribed to the pieces and their arrangement; fourthly, choose the move with the maximum evaluation. In the first programs these principles were put into practice. However, the depth of calculation was very small (four half-moves), the program did not even take exchanging operations to a conclusion, and as a result made ridiculous moves (the programs of Bernstein, de Groot, etc.).

In 1958, Newall, Simon and Shaw, well-known specialists in heuristic programming, made an attempt to get away from Shannon's first principle. They based their approach on heuristic rules, which can readily be found in a beginner's text book. Their program worked out its move, proceeding from the possibility of achieving the following six goals (in order of priority): 1. king safety, 2. material balance, 3. control over the central squares, 4. development of pieces, 5. attack on the king, and 6. advance of pawns. Associated with each goal was a set of rules for making a move, which was analysed from the viewpoint of all six goals. This program also played a weak game.

An original approach has been made by Botvinnik. He regards chess as a hierarchical control system with three levels. At the lowest level each piece operates along a certain trajectory, and has its goal of play; the next level forms groups of pieces, interacting in so-called zones of play and pursuing their goals. At the highest level the general, main goal corresponds to the aggregate of all the pieces. The goals at different levels are to a certain extent coordinated, and consist of a striving to win material. Movement along the trajectories (and their beams) enables one to calculate the "relative strengths" by means of a so-called "general exchange" operation, and thus to determine the priority move. The algorithm of play solves the problem of choosing a move in a three-stage system, and, what's more, the information taken into account is restricted by the depth of analysis (this is the so-called horizon method, and by horizon is understood a set number of half-moves). In the opinion of N. A. Krinitsky, Botvinnik's algorithm differs from Shannon's ideas mainly in that there is no static function, evaluating the position. And in general the basis of the algorithm comprises the concept not of position, but of trajectory, i.e. the possibility of moving a piece when it is one's turn to move. The trajectories and their beams "penetrate" through a large number of positions. A move is chosen along one of the trajectories in accordance with the goal of play. Botvinnik also has a move search, but for him each move is not so much a step leading from one position to another, so much as a movement along a trajectory, directed towards the achievement of the goal of play.

We think that this distinction is not especially significant. One can, evidently, construct an algorithm on Shannon's principles, and it will be equivalent to Botvinnik's algorithm. Botvinnik criticizes Shannon's approach, based on maximization of the evaluation function, for the fact that "the piece elements of one colour do not have their individual goals; their goals are impersonal, and coincide exactly with the goal of play of the sum of the elements", as a result of which, supposedly, "in the process of selecting a move it (the piece) must be moved in all directions, and its movement acquires a chaotic character" (cf. M. M. Botvinnik: "O Kiberneticheskoi Tseli Igry" ("Cybernetic Goals of Play"), p. 26, *Soviet Radio*, *Moscow*, 1975.) To us this criticism does not appear sufficiently convincing. At the same time it is obvious that Botvinnik has suggested successful solutions for organizing informational blocks for calculation, and also for other standard programming problems. As Botvinnik himself remarks, in finishing his algorithm and realizing his program he has encountered serious difficulties. For this reason it is as yet very difficult to evaluate the strength of this algorithm.

Due to their obvious complexity, teaching principles in chess programs have not been applied. But in draughts, experiments with teaching have proved successful. A program written by A. Samuel (1967) formed good evaluation functions by the statistical analysis of examples from a draughts instruction book. In 38% of cases it chooses the move recommended in the book (a random choice would select the book move in only 12% of cases). The program learns by heart moves from the book, as well as positions which often occur in play and are given a high evaluation. This program plays excellent draughts, and once defeated the champion of the State of Connecticut, the master R. Nilli. This is how Nilli annotated his game in the magazine *IBM Research News:*

"In our game one can pick out several features. All the moves up to the 11th can be found in literature, although I several times avoided well-known continuations, in the vain hope of confusing the machine. The subsequent development of the game was highly unusual. It is interesting that, in order to win, the machine had to find several brilliant moves, and, had it not done so, I would several times have had the chance to draw the game. For this reason I continued playing. However, the machine conducted the ending of the game without a single mistake."

One of the best modern American programs, developed in 1967 by Richard Greenblatt and others, uses a lot of opening theory information and certain chess "knowledge". In it are perfected the procedures for moving through the "tree of play", it watches for repetition of position, the evaluation of moves is made for the "current", and not the "final" position, and so on. This program, under the name of *Mac Hek Six* is numbered among the honorary members of the USA Chess Federation. On 21st January 1967 it for the first time played a game in a chess tournament: true, it lost it in 55 moves to a fairly strong player (rating 2190, which corresponds roughly to a good Soviet candidate master). But a game against a player with an established rating of 1510 (an average strength amateur) ended in mate on the 21st move. This, the first game won by a computer against a human in a chess tournament, deserves to be given here:

White: *Mac Hek Six*   Black: *N. N.*

**1 e4 c5 2 d4 c×d4 3 Q×d4 Nc6 4 Qd3 Nf6 5 Nc3 g6 6 Nf3 d6 7 Bf4
e5 8 Bg3 a6 9 0—0—0 b5 10 a4 Bh6+ 11 Kb1 b4 12 Q×d6 Bd7 13 Bh4
Bg7 14 Nd5 N×e4 15 Nc7+ Q×c7 16 Q×c7 Nc5 17 Qd6 Bf8 18 Qd5
Rc8 19 N×e5 Be6 20 Q×c6+ R×c6 21 Rd8.** Mate in the style of a well-
known game by Morphy.

An improved program by Greenblatt also participated in the 1974
World Championship for computer programs.

Our *Kaissa* was developed in 1967 by a group of Moscow mathemati-
cians, G. M. Adelson-Velsky, V. L. Arlazarov, A. V. Uskov and others.
A part was played in its development by the master A. R. Bitman.
It successfully competed against the program of McCarthy, and also,
after improvements, in the 1974 Stockholm Tournament for Chess
Computers.

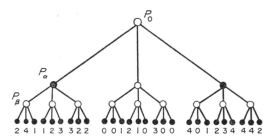

Fig. 13. Graphical representation of an algorithm in the form of a tree of play. The
white circles signify positions with White to move, and the black circles—positions
with Black to move. The numbers show evaluations of different positions.

The principles, upon which the algorithm of *Kaissa* is founded, are
not very complicated, although their programming involves many
difficulties. Let us imagine the algorithm in the form of a tree of play
(Fig. 13).[1] The initial position P_0 is regarded as the root of the tree. It is

---

[1] A detailed description of the algorithm is given in an article by G. M. Adelson-
Velsky *et al.*, "On programming a computer to play chess" *Uspekhi Matematiches-
kikh Nauk,* **XXV**, 2, 1970.

for P_0 that the best move is being sought. For this it is sufficient to evaluate all the positions which are obtained from P_0 within one move. White's goal, naturally, is to reach the concluding position with the highest evaluation, while Black's goal is the lowest. If the maximum rank of positions of the tree is equal to l (the distance from the initial apex is called the rank of the apex), then all positions of this rank are final ones. From an evaluation of these positions one can find evaluations for all possible ranks l-1, l-2 and finally, for positions of the 1st and zero ranks, which determine the best move in position P_0. The evaluation of position P_α is chosen correspondingly on the basis of the maximum (minimum) evaluation of position P_β. In this scheme the examination of each move looks identical, and as a result of the move search the evaluation of the position is determined. The block-diagram of such a search algorithm is shown in Fig. 14. In it the block "writing out of moves" determines the possible moves in a given position, and records them in a list of the not-yet-studied. The block "is there a move?" checks for the presence of at least one not-yet-studied move. "Move" makes the transition from the position under examination P_l of rank l to position P_{l+1} of rank $l+1$. If position P_{l+1} is a final one, this block determines its evaluation. If it is not a final one, motion upwards through the tree begins. The last block in the right-hand branch of the algorithm block-diagram works out the evaluation of position l, after all the moves from this position have been studied within the bounds of the search. Such an organization of the algorithm according to the "down-up" scheme enables one to reduce the volume of information necessary for making the search.

In the algorithm of our *Kaissa*, one further subtlety is employed, enabling the time on the search of positions to be reduced. In it, positions on which the evaluation of position P_0 does not depend are not examined, but are cut off. Suppose that P_α is a position with White to move, and P_β a position with Black to move, and that the partial evaluation of $P_\alpha \geqslant$ partial evaluation of P_β. Then one does not need to consider the not-yet-studied moves from position P_β, since they can only lower the evaluation of P_β, and the evaluation of P_α can only increase. It is on

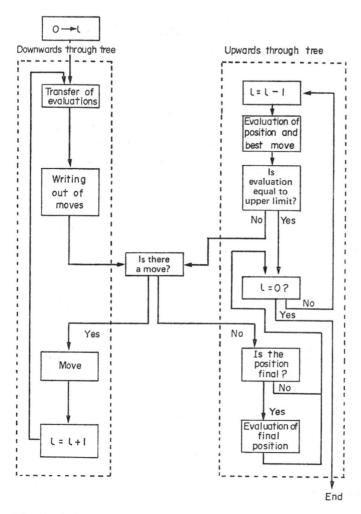

Fig. 14. Block-diagram of an algorithm of movement through the search tree

the theory of boundaries and evaluations of A. L. Brudno, which is a generalization of this idea, that the cut-off mechanism is based.

The cut-off of the stated positions is a kind of "good move service". In other words, the cut-off results in an ordering of the moves according

7

to their preliminarily established value. It is natural that if the moves are "laid out" in the correct order, a reduction in the search is achieved.

A special feature of the program is that the operation of choosing a move is as though played through on a crude model of play, on a model of chess such that preference is given to "active" moves. It is to be hoped that these active moves are not at all bad. These are in the main forcing moves, i.e. moves after which material is won (the capture of a piece, for example), or a threat is created to win material, as well as checks and replies to them. The separation of active moves enables one to limit the search depth of all remaining "quiet" moves, for example to five half-moves, while forcing moves are examined to a considerably greater depth, practically to the end. After all, even a human player hardly takes any variation as far as mate, and in hardly any position does he consider all the moves.

Practice has shown the following to be a good priority of indications by which to order the moves:

(a) in positions where material has been won, withdrawals to non-attacked squares away from the attack of the enemy piece which made the last move;

(b) promotions, favourable captures and captures on the square to which the opponent's previous move was made;

(c) the best moves and best replies, recorded in a special "guide" in accordance with computed evaluations;

(d) withdrawals away from the attack of the enemy piece which made the last move;

(e) castling and capturing *en passant*;

(f) capture of protected piece of equal value;

(g) checks on non-attacked squares;

(h) moves to non-attacked squares;

(i) moves by the king to get out of check, if the right to castle has been lost;

(j) checks on attacked squares;

(k) moves to attacked squares;

(l) moves by the king out of check, if the right to castle has not been lost.

Particular note should be taken of a feature which is reflected in the forming of the weights in the best move guide. From the viewpoint of search strategy, it is not always favourable from an intermediate position to examine first the objectively strongest chess move. It is better to try a weaker move, but one which will more quickly 'close' the search (lead more quickly to the final position). It is for this reason that, in positions where material has been won, it is better to avoid complications, which can result from the best moves in the chess sense.[2]

The concept of an active move depends on the values of the evaluation functions of this or that position. For the evaluation functions the following "material" evaluations of pieces and pawns are taken: pawn—2, knight—7, bishop—7, rook—10, queen—20. The material evaluation for the king does not exist, since the king is always present on the board. The positional evaluation function does not exceed 1 in absolute value. In concluding positions with a win for White, $f(p) = c$, with a draw $f(p) = 0$, and with a win for Black, $f(p) = -c$, where the value of c exceeds the maximum possible gain of material. The weighting of positional indications is chosen such that any combination of them cannot compensate for the minimum material advantage ("half a pawn"). Experience has shown that this is not at all bad for a small depth of search. For example, a piece standing in the centre, a rook on any open file, a passed pawn, etc., are evaluated positively, while an isolated pawn, the loss of castling, a "hole"—a square attacked by an enemy pawn and not defended by one's own pawns, have a negative weighting value.

By March 1974 the traits of a position, used for calculating the evaluation function, were expanded, and account was taken of their dependence on the type of position. In the middlegame, for example, the safety of the king is more important, so that to move it into the centre is bad, whereas in certain endgames it is essential; open files are useless if the heavy pieces have been exchanged, etc. The time for the searching of certain forcing variations was reduced, and the endgame program was

---

[2] For details of these human and computer heuristics, cf. M. V. Donskoy, "A chess-playing program" *Problemy Kibernetiki*, **29**, 1974.

improved, in particular as regards the more exact evaluation of pawn advances, and so on.

In general, *Kaissa*, as its 1974 games showed, does not play badly. The question is: can a chess program surmount the grandmaster (or master) barrier? Many, including Donald Michie, who was mentioned earlier, consider that if one were to succeed in creating such a program, it would be possible to program anything one liked. In 1968, Michie, together with McCarthy and Seymour Papert, made a bet with international master David Levy (who was, incidentally, one of the organizers of the Stockholm computer tournament) for £1000 that in 1978 the latter would lose to a chess program. At that time Botvinnik said to Levy: "I am very sorry for your money." But Michie himself thinks otherwise, and his thoughts are of interest.[3]

In chess programs, Michie considers, there is nothing that relates to the "understanding" of chess, i.e. to that knowledge which in the first instance is possessed by a human. The only knowledge that a program has relates to the rules of the game, evaluation functions and opening variations, stored in its permanent memory. But this is a mere drop in the ocean of knowledge accumulated even by an amateur. It follows that one must first and foremost find principles, by means of which the great store of knowledge can be presented to the machine in forms which make possible a process of generalization, associative thinking and expanding of knowledge by learning. Thus the question of the "grandmaster" barrier turns into the question of how to represent chess knowledge in machine form.

Michie thinks that, instead of a tree of play, its description can be given in a different, more compact form, in the form of a "semantic graph", the structure of which approximates to the image of the position with which a human works. Such a graph is depicted in Figure 15. Then the program will chiefly recognize images, and this is already a step forward. Then the present-day "mechanized ignoramuses", calculating trees with half a million evaluated positions, would be inferior to programs which

---

[3] Levy won his bet in 1978 by defeating the American program *Chess* in a match of six games (K. P. N.).

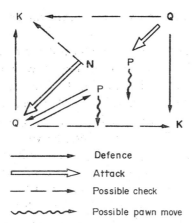

------------▶   Defence

═════════▷   Attack

— · — · —▶   Possible check

∿∿∿∿∿▷   Possible pawn move

Fig. 15. "Semantic graph" of the position given earlier in Fig. 2. White's pieces and possible actions are shown in heavy type, those of Black in ordinary type.

"understand the play", working on the basis of principles, close to human vision and thinking. Therefore the progress on the path to the grandmaster barrier lies in changing the very principles, stemming from Shannon, of a formal description of the game of chess.

We do not know whether Michie is right, and what will be the speed of progress along this new path. No doubt this path to the electronic grandmaster will also be long and difficult.

As confirmation of this, we give certain ideas of the great American neuro-cyberneticist Hubert Dreyfus. He points out that in all the main directions of work on artificial intelligence (programming of games, machine translation and image recognition), the optimistic forecasts of the nineteen fifties have been replaced by disillusionment and a slowing down in the tempo of research. The more qualitatively complicated the problem, the more clearly are the limitations of the electronic computer revealed. This limitation is a result of the strict formalization of methods of processing information in the computer. The mind of a human also uses a formalized approach, but at the same time it is also capable of qualitatively different analysis methods. The ability to fulfil non-formalized operations, in the opinion of Dreyfus, ensures success where a discrete search or review of alternatives, based even on the most clever heuristics, proves helpless.

To some extent the thinking of a chess player reduces to the analysis of discrete possibilities, to the checking of variations, bringing man close to a machine, but this checking begins—and it is important to emphasize this—with an action which is not determined by such checking. At the source of checking, as has been shown by the psychological experiments of Herbert Simon and others, lie vague, unlimited, at times altogether unrecognizable, promptings of "peripheral consciousness". In the thinking of a chess player processes of two kinds occur: first a drawing of the attention to a certain zone of the board, the arising of a difficult-to-prove, vague "suspicion" that it is here that there is a weak point in the opponent's position (feelings of the type: "here he seems to have some difficulties, I must strike here"), and only then—a clearly conscious checking of the possible alternatives. Probably the orientation towards the products of activity and "peripheral consciousness", so characteristic of a human and inaccessible to a machine, makes the level of work of the human brain unattainable for a computer; this relates fully to the modelling of the game of chess and to the functioning of recognition mechanisms in problem solving.

Perhaps a closer and more tangible improvement of the chess program will be "consultative play", when a human will act as assistant to a machine. We have reversed the usual formula, merely for the sake of convenience; it could, of course, be the other way round. Then a player would use the computer for an expanded and skilful analysis of variations, chosen on the basis of his knowledge and intuition, for the testing of strategic ideas, and for controlling mistakes. This would add at least 500 points on the rating scale of professor Élő. Of course, this would be a different sort of chess, more like play-cum-research, an instrument of cognition of human and artificial intelligence.

To conclude our short essay on the state of affairs and ideas in the field of computer chess, we should like to recall a splendid idea of Norman Weiner. To be a strong player, a program must possess playing individuality, a part of which, possibly, it will have to copy from its opponent. Its evaluation functions must be subject to continuous reassessment, and as a result of this "the playing automaton will be continuously transformed into some machine which differs from the intitial one in accordance with *the history of the developing play*" [our italics— *the authors*]. But will this playing automaton with its pronounced and varying individuality be a machine? Perhaps it should be called a human...?

Now, so as to digress slightly from this tiresome discussion about chess programs, we give an extract from a satirical article by Fritz Leiber 'The 64-square Mad House' published in *Canadian Chess Chat*, March and April 1965. The article describes a certain tournament, made up of nine top grandmasters and a Machine. The Machine loses three games, one of them as follows:

"In the third round Lysmov[4] defeated the Machine in 27 moves. Commotion broke out in the hall. Newsmen rushed to the phones. Everyone was analysing the game, and it was clear that Lysmov had done something tricky."

"The general emotional reaction in America, as reflected by the newspapers, was not too happy. One read between the lines that for the Machine to beat a man was bad, but for a Russian to beat an American machine was worse. [Don't forget that the year is 1965—*the authors*.] A widely-read sports columnist, two football coaches, and several rural politicians announced that chess was a morbid game played only by weirdies...."

One of the grandmasters competing against the Machine, Doctor Krakatower, gives the following explanation of Lysmov's win:

"He determined the limiting depth of calculation available to the Machine—10 moves... Lysmov played a combination in which the Machine would win his queen on the tenth move, but on the second move after these ten the Machine would be mated. A human chess master would have seen a trap like that, but the Machine could not, because Lysmov was manoeuvring in an area that did

---

[4] The author of the story has changed slightly the names of certain well-known grandmasters.

not exist for the Machine's perfect but limited mind. Of course the Machine changed its tactics after first three moves, but by that time it was too late. Lysmov was the first of us to realize fully that we are not playing against a metal monster, but against a certain kind of programming, in which weaknesses can be found."

After this the Machine won several games in a row, and became the tournament leader.

"Interest in the tournament increased sharply. The audiences grew in size and in expensiveness of wardrobe. It became a problem to maintain order in the hall.... The number of scientists and computer men in attendance increased. Navy, Army and Space Force uniforms were more in evidence. The firm WBM received a big order from the War Department. Hollywood revealed plans for two chess movies: "They Made Her a Black Pawn" and "The Monster from King Rook Square"...."

In its game with Krakatower, who on his 31st move was intending to resign,

"the Machine broke down. The programmer's assistants sprang lightly into action, filing around the back of the console. The Machine's clock ticked on. Doctor Krakatower watched for a while, and then fell asleep. When the Tournament Director jogged him awake, the Machine had just made its next move, but the repair job had taken 50 minutes. As a result the Machine had to make 15 moves in 10 minutes. At 40 seconds a move it played like a dub. Several moves later Krakatower apologetically announced mate in four."

"Oh, what an ironic glory the gods reserved for Krakatower's dotage—to vanquish a broken-down computer! Only one good thing about it—that it didn't happen while it was playing one of the Russians, or someone would surely have whispered *sabotage*."

The Machine lost a third game to the American Angler. The latter had noticed that the Machine was playing openings in exact accordance with the latest edition of a book compiled by the author of the program, the well-known former grandmaster Great [in the portrait of the program author one can recognize grandmaster Fine—*the authors*]. In one of the opening variations, Angler had discovered a blunder by Great, and had played this opening against the Machine. Soon he had put it in a hopeless position.

Thus Fritz Leiber indicated three possibilities for beating the Machine: an insufficiently deep calculation of a forcing variation, a technical fault, and an error in the opening library stored in the program. All three defects can in principle be removed.

In general, the author of the story paints a perfectly plausible picture of the future, and he depicts faithfully the characteristic traits of the players. In perhaps just one respect he allows his imagination to run wild. He endows the Machine with feelings, which it will be unlikely to possess. On winning against the Hungarian grandmaster, the Machine produced an inscription above the board: "Thank you for a good game.", and a second later added: "You had bad luck.". And when the Machine lost to Krakatower due to a fault, the following words lit up on the board: "You played brilliantly. Congratulations!"

CHAPTER 7.

Chess in the Third Millennium

THUS, we have attempted to examine chess from different aspects, to study the separate facets of this unique phenomenon, and have been seeking the key to chess creativity. But today our path to the understanding of chess is only just beginning. What awaits us tomorrow?

To us, chess players, this is not an idle question. Man always wants to know that future civilization will take even a part of his individual creativity, and that his work and talent will not be discarded from the board of progress like some pawn no longer needed in a chess game. And we wish today to see the main paths of chess development, and reflect on what new forms it can take, what sort of interest it will provoke, what role—and this is the most important—it will begin to play in a harmonious and happy world.

The authors, of course, have a boundless love for chess, and believe that by the year 2000, or perhaps even earlier, chess will have become more humane, and with each year will acquire more and more the very best features, gradually losing everything else which is temporary, alien, opportunist and foreign to the ideals of humanism.

Talking of the future, we have inevitably assumed some elements of the fantastic. And, perhaps, it is this very interference of imagination which lends a special attraction to constructed pictures of the future. Let us begin with the fact that the demands of our intellectual development, but not that of the computer, are bound to lead to a considerable growth of interest in chess. While today a child is taught basic logical concepts and relationships using empirical observations of living nature, it will be different in the world of the third millennium, where, using visual chess plans, a child in its first few months after birth will be shown logical concepts. Everyone will understand that a beautiful chess idea "beats" in the three-dimensional space of children's blocks and pyramids. Using different-coloured pieces it will be possible to encompass the whole range of ideas and feelings of a chess player, representing even the most complex of them by a few basic symbols, visible or different to the touch. With pride for chess we will say that, while simple mathematical theorems will not always do for earthly or cosmic communications, in the third millennium a set of technical chess devices and simple combinations will be understandable to any person on the Earth, and also, undoubtedly, to those on other planets. If we were in the place of those sending colour signals into the distant cosmos, we would consider anchoring ourselves on the vast wastes of the ocean both to the theorem of Pythagoras, and to the elementary "scholar's mate". We think that the concepts of forward, backward, up, down, left, right, together, separately, from corner to corner, attack, defence, late, early, reality, illusion, boldness, cowardice, quickly, slowly, risk, calculation, generously, sparingly, elementary, vulgar, beautiful, ugly, stupid, clever and certain others can be perfectly well conveyed using chess symbols, since the combination of six pieces of two colours plus pawns is countless. It goes without saying that, in our passion as authors, we realize that this is a matter not even of the coming century, but, to be honest, if in our artless striving for knowledge we wish to find a "common language" with dolphins, why shouldn't we learn to speak amongst ourselves using a square board of 64 little squares and 32 little pieces? Man is capable of anything!

Today, masterpieces of architecture and painting, music and poetry, achievements in sport and in life help the young generation to foster in itself the best features of man's future. And chess? Doesn't it carry in itself an emotional tint of personal participation in each chess action, doesn't it expand the limits of the mind in one second for 100 years back and 100 years forward? In search of a solution our mind tosses ceaselessly about both in time and in space, striving to unite the knowledge and experience of players who have long since passed away or who live on the other side of the earth, trying to guess and anticipate a future idea. Each chess game not only preserves in itself a particle of common knowledge, but for the players it is an indelible personal micro-recollection. Mixing with other colourful phenomena of a man's life, these recollections over the course of his whole life comprise a distinctive kaleidoscope, rearranging and strengthening certain recollections, suppressing and moving aside others, rewarding the memory and punishing it. Here there is a certain narcotic element, and sometime in the future chess will be used for the control of mental illness, but already now for youths it often creates an illusion of being grown up, and for old people—an illusion of continuing growth.

Chess is in itself obvious in appearance, but its depth is inexhaustible. Today we still do not yet know of a single chess player, and that includes the World Champion, who, on making his first move, could record on magnetic tape all the possible variations as he sees them. But if the best chess players in the world were to play with microphones in their hands, everyone would be able to hear how beautifully they think. However, FIDE has not even guessed that, were it to organize a tournament of talking grandmasters, the federation would gather a grateful audience of millions. (Then you would be unable to conceal your own helplessness behind someone else's moves.) In such tournaments, with the aid of television technology, masters would be able to talk to the public in the language of chess symbols. Such play, apart from anything else, would remove from the contestants a certain coating of inferiority complex, since the public consider a move which is unexpected to them to be also unexpected to the grandmaster. But with closer contact, the audience would itself fantasize less, and would penetrate more closely into the work of highly-qualified and creative thinking. As you see, the future is closing up closely on the present. . . .

In addition, no-one will bother to spend 5 hours sitting in the auditorium—during this time one can fly from Moscow to Yerevan and back, or have a dip in the Black Sea. In rapid, dynamic, attractively striking play will be conceived the main thing in chess art—improvization, the finding literally in a few minutes or even seconds of that best path, which leads from one situation to another. And along this narrow path the spectator and listener will be led by the artist.

It is highly probable that, in time, some publishing firm will bring out a game of "chess tests". Different positions will appear in an aperture for a certain time, and a control counter will indicate the score depending on the swiftness of choice of solution. The authors know that, in the Kiev Radio Engineering Technical College, one of the teachers, B. S. Gershunsky, has constructed and successfully tested this method of programming chess pleasure.

And even so, the future of chess art is seen rather differently by the authors.

Let us imagine that, in the not-too-distant future, in our country, and then abroad, there begin to open, one after another, theatres for chess performances. They already practically exist... in Yugoslavia, where travel firms have made chess an important feature of advertisement, and readily allot funds to chess events, if only to hit the headlines, to distinguish themselves in the eyes of potential tourists and to get onto the list of world travel firms. In these chess theatres it will be possible to give performances on any topic and to show creative portraits of chess players. Over the past 200 years, so much chess material has been accumulated that an experienced director in collaboration with a composer would for at least 1000 years be able to compose thematic concerts. And if new authors should appear, or the old authors should bring their re-shaped satires—be honest now, you've never seen or heard on the stage a specifically chess satire—then, as you yourself realize, there will be no lack of actors wishing to appear in the roles of Paul Morphy, Mikhail Botvinnik, Howard Staunton or Henrique Mecking.

In such a theatre one can synchronously show the outstanding games of the day, receiving the moves by wire or by TV channel. One can show matches played in other towns over 20, 40 or 100 boards. One can hold quizzes and problem-solving competitions. There would be much that chess players could devise, if they didn't just have a crowded private house for administration on Gogol Boulevard, but their own Chess Building.

In such a building there will be a publishing house and special schools for all ages, there will be a cinema for showing examples of chess creativity, and a historical hall, where one will see the smile of Capablanca, and there can be a hall for simultaneous displays whit a live grandmaster or an electronic computer. (The authors realize that actual projects mature simultaneously in the minds of different people. And it is pleasant for us to find among like thinkers N. Nosov, the author of *Neznaiki v Solnechnom Gorodye* (The Dunces in the Sunny Town).

Colour TV cassettes will be produced there, with the best creative games of the World Champions. They will have sound, and it will be possible to listen in parallel to commentaries either by the players, or by other experts.

There will be for hire portable chess computers, in whose memories will be recorded everything possible about chess. Players will use this information even during tournament games, so as not to overload their own memories, thereby retaining their strength for genuinely creative effort. And so on, and so forth.

...Children will listen to an explanatory text to the games, as today they listen to the story of *Little Red Riding Hood*. Present-day examples of chess art, over which we still from time to time go into raptures, will provoke mistrust in them, and our mistakes will seem to them to be terrible stupidities, because they will know these outmoded, naïve old moves. But they will also know that the very best players did not play at their maximum strength, if their methods, their play, their ideas brought them success. For this reason it is senseless to talk about the matches Morphy–Karpov, Capablanca–Anderssen, or Philidor–Tal. After all, both in the past, and in the present, each perfects his mastery only to the limits of victory. There is also another factor—it is dangerous to extend very far if the critics do not understand a player. Usually at such a boundary are the World Champions. They do not explain how they win, not wishing to reveal their secrets. And so there is present a definite gap between new methods of solving complex problems and their interpretation by journalists and commentators. Chess has hardly become more complex. If the number of masters is growing amazingly rapidly, doesn't this mean that it is too easy to play chess today! Are we not deceiving ourselves and the public? Any subject is interesting, if you spend on it the length of time it deserves. If today dozens of grand-masters and hundreds of masters can play an excellent game within only 5 minutes, it means that they have up their sleeve certain prepared schemes for all basic instances, just as any person in many even new situations orients himself in transit. They say that there is no time to calculate variations. But is that what chess is—the calculation of varia-tions? Fine thinks that the strength of the great Champions was that they created highly complex situations, rich in possibilities, the calcula-tion of which was impossible, and that they nevertheless found a way out from them, while their opponents cried "it's all up!", and waited for extraneous assistance.

What else will there be in the chess of the future? Chess theatres will invite top-class grandmasters to make tours. Their top-class will be ex-pressed in their speed of problem solving, and they will be in the nature of conjurer-intellectuals. They will display miracles of intuition and the logical working of the brain, will provoke admiration, but will not ex-perience negative emotions—their work will be respected for itself, and not in dependence on the result of a game. They will be greeted by the audience, just as a soloist and orchestra are today, and not as conqueror and conquered.

Tournaments and matches in their present-day sense will fade into the past. Only occasionally, as a curiosity, will competitions be ar-ranged—picnics, where spectators will be allowed to behave as in the "good old days", the contestants will arrive for a round, not knowing what opening the opponent has planned and on what they will have to hold a discussion, the controllers will force them to keep a score of the game and of the number of moves, and the chess pieces themselves will be hidden from the spectators by the massive walls of the chess clocks, the demonstration will be with the help of long poles, picking up the pieces and hanging them on nails, and for the younger spectators this entire carnival will be merely a lesson on the history of the origin of chess art.

The person of the future will be economical in the expenditure of his "self" and of his individual time, said Emanuel Lasker in his *Chess*

Manual. Therefore, in chess theatres, in the evening or in the morning, at night or, perhaps, during the day, chess concerts will be held. The programs will be announced beforehand, and everyone will come along to watch or listen to the topic which he finds interesting. Those wishing to test their strength against grandmasters will no longer play with live opponents—they can well be replaced by computers. But they will play only for general pleasure in an atmosphere of promptings and exchange of jokes. They will devise mystery displays, where the spectators have to guess which one of the grandmasters is playing. There was recently something similar in Nice at the Chess Olympiad, where the master Filiber, under the mask of an automaton, readily strode to and forth. But in the future they will simply insert into a genuine automaton a cassette, which in the characteristic manner of the grandmaster in question will quickly or slowly "think" at the critical points of the game, sacrifice or capture pawns and pieces, aim for the endgame or avoid it. The cassette will introduce live creative traits into the working of the automaton. Who will resolve into schemes the styles of Tal, Botvinnik or Karpov? This will be a job for other specialized computers, since for a long time this will not be within the powers of people.

A central automatic service of the Chess Building will be formed, and you will be able to link up to a computer by telephone and play against it, or—if you wish—an entire family. After the game, together with a bill for the electricity, the computer will send you a copy of the game. Out of several games a collection can be made, and, comparing it with a collection of games by Grandad, you can rejoice that, although the strength of the grandchild is less than that of his grandad, the computer is improving from one tournament to the next. Because computer championships will be just as natural as running is today, and machine experience will become common property.

In our attempt to look into the future, features of the present come distinctly to the fore. This is inevitable, we realize this, perhaps it is only the emotional pitch of our writing which confuses these features to a slightly greater extent that the carping reader would like. We beg the reader to be tolerant.

In the future, perhaps, new forms of chess will appear. We consider here only chess phenomena, stemming from classical chess, as it is "formalized" today, and will not bother to talk about the dozens of varieties of this game, devised by enthusiasts, although we realize the lawfulness of many changes. But we will make one exception. Out of respect for the person of Albert Einstein, who some 40 years ago suggested that a third dimension should be introduced into chess. It is a pity that this innovation has not been tried in practice. It would be interesting to organize a grandmaster tournament in the Einstein Institute in Paris. If certain pieces could in one move, others gradually—through the sides of the board—move into space, the game could become enthralling, the spectators would be arranged on any side, and the demonstration of games would require apparatus of the sort which operates in a planetarium.

On the other hand, today chess sets themselves need at least to be brought into a general form—in different countries they differ in colour, size, form, weight, size of squares on the board, and so on. Common international unification is required. In little more than a year, after all, the publishers of *Informator* created an international language for chess players. This is an uncommon occurrence, and the language itself does not have a logical basis, but games in it are not only published, but also read. People pick up easy reading matter, not thinking, however, too much about the squares and circles, which do not have anything in common with those high symbols about which we were reflecting at the beginning of this chapter.

Changes touch first and foremost on the modern means of communicating moves onto demonstration boards. Some 20 years ago a little-known inventor, living in a remote little German village, devised a simple magnetic method for automatically reproducing moves on a large demonstration screen. But neither this invention, nor a later one on the theme of "synchronous transmission of moves and calculation of time used," has come into practice. Some enthusiasts from Perm University have developed an electronic demonstration board, which is excellent, but the only specimen of it is flaunted in the Central Chess Club. Obviously its cost is beyond the means of the Chess Federation.

In the future the position will change radically. In the theatres there will be enormous coloured demonstration boards. Alongside will be smaller boards, on which the grandmasters will be able to demonstrate their plans, helping the spectator to understand and experience the play. The pieces and pawns will float smoothly across from square to square. They will gradually fade on their departure square, their shadow will accompany the path of their movement, then their image will gradually emerge in a new place. The knight too will make a visible move along the edge of the squares. The pieces of the side which has made a move will assume a relaxed pose, whereas the entire appearance of the opponent's pieces will indicate concentration of mental effort and intensity of feeling. Possibly the pieces will acquire the form of living beings, and in each piece will be something unusual. Say, a little pocket, out of which captured pawns stare, or with an indication of the number of moves and time spent on a particular piece. The squares of the board will be illuminated from behind, so as to avoid tiring the eyes. Here one can fantasize to one's heart's content....

The new forms and style of "active" demonstration will lead to a situation where, during a big tournament, the hall will be transformed to dimensions of fantastic size. Spectators will be completely absorbed in the chess, they will cease to experience time and space, their predictions will race a century forward, and each move on the stage will provoke associations with champions and creative players of past eras. And it is in this that chess will be significantly distinguished from any other activity, in which we experience a feeling of co-experience. Because here there is also a process of collective creativity, which often reaches intellectual ecstasy: the entire auditorium is agitated, burning and working like a single large human computer. It is a pity that at present this collective computer has already swallowed some fifteen to twenty initial moves, putting back the boundary at which genuine creativity begins.

In the future it is unlikely that an institution which is so alien to chess as the press centre will be retained. This amateur organization has imperceptibly acquired for itself the right arrogantly to criticize any idea, plan, move, attack or defence of the grandmasters in action. When an important match is in progress, there congregate in it dozens of grandmasters, and hundreds of journalists with a slight experience of criticism. They not only follow the play, they themselves heatedly play, endlessly moving the pieces about on dozens of subsidiary boards, attempting gropingly to reach the finish of this or that combination. And then the readers are presented with the statement: "All of us in the press centre saw that it was necessary not to play this, but that." And, of course, it can happen that this international brain centre, compressed into one room, begins to defeat those doing battle on the stage. And what a good thing it is that the public are not admitted in here from the auditorium—they would lose their respect for the live champions, they would forget that the latter are thinking tirelessly in positions, which are not on the board itself, nor on the demonstration boards, since the art of playing chess is the art of prognostication, and not of groping. After all, if even three spectators should together ponder over a single pocket set, they gain the chance of rising level with the grandmasters playing on the stage. It is worth reflecting on this phenomenon. Often we read how some little boy in the hall made himself happy, and also his parents—he guessed Tal's move.... In the press centre they also guess. It would be interesting if FIDE was to set up a totalizer in the press centre....

But these problems exist. Especially if one takes into account the competitive fervour of a game, the cruel intellectual slaughter, the fact that three or six times a week grandmasters must not only endure a brain-storm with a critical mark and find ways of rapidly re-establishing the normal functions of the organism, but also at any rate to seek ways of living normally for all the remaining part of their non-chess life. Not all cope with equally well. Some become depressed, others excessively cheerful, and a third set begin throwing stones at the glass house in which they themselves not long ago were blooming and in a state of bliss. However, the percentage of such deviations is not more than 10—the norm for any form of well-paid and extremely dangerous human activity. Nevertheless, in the future all this will change for the better, since envy and malevolence will disappear, so that there will be no need either for pity, or for charitable laudatory comments, of which today we are all so fond. Here there is also another aspect.

Imperturbable players like Karpov, who practically makes no reaction to the hall—"the public does not interest me"—retain a high degree of work capacity longer than their less composed opponents. Or take Fischer: the public affected him, but he found a defence to this—he restricted the range of problems in the opening, and such play enabled him by simple means to solve complex problems. Karpov also plays the opening in simple fashion, and builds his subsequent play on the technical exploitation of positional gains. Thus as a whole it turns out that the best results are achieved by players who are talented, with excellent health, nerves of steel, and will-power.

Another problem concerns methods of play. Theorists have to predict the strategy of tomorrow, proceeding from the fact today 99 per cent of games are a cardiogram of a struggle, a cardiogram of the efforts of an individual in his struggle not only with the difficulties of the position, but also with himself, with the clock, with the noise in the hall, and so on. Here no progress is apparent—and this worries all lovers of chess. It is good to resemble Morphy, but it is even better to guess the strategy of the twenty-first century and to be victorious, as Morphy himself was victorious, by guessing the progress of the game a century in advance.

What are needed are boldness and passion, the desire and the ability to proceed towards an as yet unclear goal, and only this gives rise to sparkling positions and highly dynamic, deep situations. Here each player, on the basis of his mental experience, experiences chess emotions, creating new chess ideas, expressed in plans and moves. With passion of this sort, dry, academically correct and short-lived variations will remain to one side, but this is the charm of genuine creativity: to take on one's shoulders a barely visible, lengthy series of subtle moves, which within a short time—speed of perception for the spectators—will show man's inherent vision.

Some 30 years ago, Reuben Fine, a great lover of blindfold chess, and especially at speed—10 seconds a move, and 10 games in this way, one after another—said that although this was difficult, it was interesting; that the ability to play, without looking at the board, serves as an intellectual standard for chess players. Philidor, who played 3 games blindfold, found his way into the British Encyclopaedia, while today the world record is held by János Flesch—52. And what of the future? There is, after all, the computer, destined to rid man of routine work and free his brain for creative matters. Under these conditions there is no necessity to train him to remember the positions, glimpsed kaleidoscopically and fleetingly during blindfold play. For this reason blindfold play is unlikely to receive any new stimuli. Provided, of course, that this art form does not interest the circus. Fine's ideas have been justified in another way. A more subtle evaluation has appeared of those positions, which are apparently neither interesting, nor presenting any basis for playing for a win. The best players in the world, Karpov, Fischer, Larsen, Spassky and Tal, although they do not give blindfold displays, are able to see far beyond the bounds of the visible position. The only difficulty on this lengthy path is, like a racing cyclist, not to lose courage and strength, and to maintain one's character against the enormous resistance of the opponent.

But today in tournaments, the one who wins is often not the one who constructs long-range plans, but he who simply fights move by move. These players have no disappointments, because they do not seek the maximum, except that they digest the maximum amount of chess information. This is rationalism. Players are prepared to repeat old positions, provided they bring success.

If you wish to possess a knowledge of the mechanics leading to a win, you must understand that around which the struggle is proceeding, at what the defence is directed, and where is the target of attack. But there is much more to it than that. One requires enthusiasm, fantasy, willpower, searching, a craving to find the true solution in one's rivalry with another individual. When there is all this—a chess genius emerges. Morphy played easily, beautifully and quickly. He understood positions, and had an excellent sense of the relationships of their details. But he valued very highly the spark of fantasy, of initiative. On this path Morphy was invincible, but he was also unhappy, because there was no-one with whom to share the happiness of his discovery, no-one understood the deep sources of his play, his creative enthusiasm. Today there is a public which is capable of understanding and evaluating discovery in chess. But chess players do not play for the public. Today there is an endless competition. After winning today, even so tomorrow you will again be tested... on the strength of your health and the work capacity of your talent. Just that!

...The authors believe that in the third millennium chess will finally enter into the range of man's life necessities, along with the reading of the classics and the enjoyment of music....

Possibly one minute in the life of a man may be devoted to chess, but we will be proud even of such an achievement; a compressed minute of the future is thought by us to be equal in capacity and depth to a present day century, or even more.

In the future the world will probably be divided, not only into men and women, but also into people and machines. Anyone wishing to make an objective assessment of the progress of chess in the past 100 years should look through magazines and old newspapers. A chess "revolution" is at hand—from the primitive we have reached a summit of intellect. At the same time confidence is growing in the unrealized dream of the chess player who does not lose. This will only be within the capacity of a machine, since the number of reasonable chess positions, arrived at in reasonable, even if many, ways, is nevertheless finite and is subject both to research and to systemization. But we should like to see how to the building of the former Moscow Conservatoire (the 1940 USSR Championship was played there), handed over to a theatre of chess productions, computers drive up on their own wheels or air cushions, staidly enter the building, leave their means of rapid propulsion at the cloak room, and take their seats according to rank. Such a chess evening there will undoubtedly be, the computers will also want to observe the play of their live rivals, gain experience, criticize a little, mix with one another, and finally, to make one another's acquaintance, to establish bonds of creative affection, of personal friendship, and to arrange useful work contacts. They wink lamps, move switches and knobs, gain mutual pleasure, and, on leaving the theatre, gossip as people do nowadays, and exchange punched cards to call up one another. See how poor the human imagination is—we see everything in our own manner. Or perhaps we will even ask the most famous computers for their autographs and for bits of components as souvenirs.... But it will be some time before machines are able to imitate the play of live people, and the creative life of the live champions will for a long time yet continue to shine, serving the cognition of chess secrets.

In conclusion, the authors beg the reader not to complain of the exaggeration and the sharpness of our assessment of the present day. This is a difficult topic. There are people who altogether disclaim chess as an art, but then are there only a few who also disclaim art in general? We will not take it upon ourselves to judge them, we can only feel regret for those who are deaf and blind to the wonderful world of chess.

Index of Individuals Mentioned in the Text

Nimzowitsch, Aron (1886–1935)   75 (Latvian-born grandmaster, one of the greatest chess innovators and most profound writers on the game).

Paustovsky, Konstantin (1892–1968)   32 (Russian short story writer and journalist).

Petrosian, Tigran (1929–   )   35, 54, 71–2, 76, 78 (Soviet grandmaster, World Champion (1963–69).

Philidor, François (1726–1795)   100, 106 (French, the leading player of the 18th century).

Polugayevsky, Lyev (1934–   )   8 (Soviet grandmaster, one of the world's leading players over the past decade).

Prokofiev, Sergey (1891–1953)   23 (Russian composer and pianist).

Pushkin, Aleksandr (1799–1837)   72 (Russia's greatest poet, also dramatist, novelist and short story writer).

Ragozin, Vyacheslav (1908–1962)   52 (Soviet grandmaster, theorist and writer).

Reshevsky, Samuel (1911–   )   56 (Polish-born American grandmaster, child prodigy, for many years the strongest Western player).

Reti, Richard (1889–1929)   10, 31 (Czech grandmaster, fine writer and endgame study composer).

Rubinstein, Akiba (1882–1961)   71 (Polish-born grandmaster, profound openings innovator and endgame expert).

Saint-Exupery, Antoine de (1900–1944)   48 (French novelist, essayist and aviator).

Shannon, Claude   40, 81–3, 91 (1916–   ) (One of the great American pioneers in the development and application of electronic computing).

Shukshin, Vasily (1929–1974)   18 (Soviet writer, actor and film director).

Smejkal, Jan (1946–   )   56 (Czech grandmaster).

Smyslov, Vasily (1921–   )   63, 64, 65, 93 (Soviet grandmaster, World Champion 1957–58).

Spassky, Boris (1937–   )   53, 54, 70, 71, 78, 107 (Soviet grandmaster, World Champion 1969–72).

Spielmann, Rudolf (1883–1942)   35, 72 (Austrian grandmaster).

Staunton, Howard (1810–1874)   99 (English, the world's leading player in the 1840s).

Steinitz, Wilhelm (1836–1900)   6, 7, 69 (First official World Champion, 1886–94, the first player to give chess a scientific basis).

Suetin, Alexei (1926–   )   35 (Soviet grandmaster and prominent chess writer).

Swift, Jonathan (1667–1745)   37 (English satirist, poet, political writer and clergyman).

Szabó, László (1917–   )   72 (Hungarian grandmaster, for many years his country's leading player).

Tal, Mikhail (1936–   )   9, 32, 44, 51, 66, 70, 71, 74, 78, 100, 102, 105, 107 (Soviet grandmaster, World Champion 1960–61, one of the greatest attacking players, penetrating writer on the game).